Authors in Their Age

CHAUCER

Authors in Their Age

CHAUCER

Gillian Evans

BLACKIE

BLACKIE & SON LTD.
Bishopbriggs Glasgow G64 2NZ
450 Edgware Road London W2 1EG

© Gillian Evans 1977
First Published 1977
Educational edition ISBN 0 216 90184 7
General edition ISBN 0 216 90192 8

Filmset in Ireland by
Doyle Photosetting Ltd., Tullamore.
Printed in Great Britain by
Robert Maclehose & Co. Ltd., Glasgow.

Authors in Their Age

Authors in Their Age is a series of introductions to the work of major authors in English literature. Each book provides the background information that can help a reader see such an author in context, involved in and reacting to the society of which he was a part.

Some volumes are devoted to individual authors such as Chaucer and Wordsworth. Others look at a particular period in our literary history in which an author can be seen as representative of his time— for example, *The Age of Keats and Shelley* and *The Age of Lawrence*.

There is no attempt to impose a standard format on each of the books. However, all the books provide biographical material and deal with the important political, social and cultural movements of the time. Each book considers the author's readership, the problems of editing his or her work and the major influences on his or her writing. All are well illustrated with drawings, documents or photographs of the time.

There is also a guide to further reading and other source material which will enable the student to progress to a more detailed study of the writer's work and its treatment by literary critics.

Anthony Adams
Esmor Jones
General Editors

Contents

I

Towards a Biography of Chaucer

Chaucer left no systematic record of his life: nor did any contemporary tell his story; biography was almost unknown in the 14th century. Of his mind and character, his tastes and interests, we know only what the poems tell us; of the events of his life there remain only small hints in diplomatic and legal documents of the period. But the details which do survive evoke a picture of a recognizable human being, with a career and a family, business worries and, at times, a fair degree of success in the civil service and at court. Chaucer wrote in the time he could spare from a busy life.

1. This familiar portrait of Chaucer may be closer to life than many medieval pictures of well-known figures. In *The Canterbury Tales* the pilgrim Chaucer appears as a portly figure; the Host says: '*He in the waast is shape as wel as I*', and we know from Chaucer's description that the Host is himself '*a large man*'. The portrait shows Chaucer as a confident man of the world. (BM Harley 4866)

Nearly five hundred contemporary documents have been found in which Chaucer's name appears, or which have some close connection with him or with his immediate family. Almost every kind of 14th century record which might contain references to him has been explored but it is not impossible that there are more examples. In most of these documents Chaucer is no more than a name; the story of his life has had to be pieced together from fragmentary hints as to the post he held, or the journey he undertook, at a particular time. It was only in 1966 that M. M. Crow and C. C. Olson published the *Chaucer Life Records* which contain most of the known material. A full biography of Chaucer, based on these documents, has yet to be written; but it will inevitably be full of questions and speculation; we shall never have more than an outline of Chaucer's full and active life.

Chaucer was born into the administrative classes, at a time when they were growing more powerful and influential. There was no rigid barrier between the middle classes and the aristocracy, in England at least. Chaucer's father was a London wine-merchant of some standing, and he was able to give his son a good start in life by getting him a place in the royal household. Chaucer served first as a page in the household of Elizabeth, Countess of Ulster, the wife of Lionel, Duke of Clarence, third son of Edward III. It is in the Countess's household accounts for 1357 that we find the first mention of Chaucer: '*To Geoffrey Chaucer of London on the 20th day of May this year, 2s.*'[1] And at Christmas, 1357, a gift: '*for necessities against the feast.*'[2]

If Chaucer went to school, it may have been to St Paul's School where he would have learnt Latin and studied the classical poets; he would have been taught little else.

When Edward III went campaigning in France in 1359–60, in the hope of asserting his claim to the French crown, Chaucer was evidently old enough to accompany the army. Probably he was in his late teens at this time. He was held prisoner until March 1360, when he was ransomed with other captives. The king must have valued his services enough to contribute sixteen pounds to his ransom. The Earl of Ulster found him sufficiently trustworthy to use as a messenger during the peace negotiations in October 1360. Chaucer's career was, it seems, already prospering.

There follows a gap of seven years, during which we can only suppose that Chaucer continued in the royal service and made himself useful to his masters unless, as has been suggested, he studied law at the Inns of Court. Then he was sent abroad on a mission. He was given a passport and ten pounds travelling expenses, but we do not know where he went, or the purpose of his journey. He had by now a royal pension of twenty marks (a mark = 13s 4d) for life, given him by Edward III in 1367. In 1370 the King gave him letters of protection when he sent him on another journey: '*Geoffrey Chaucer who is about to go overseas in the service of the King, has the King's letter of protection.*'³ He evidently proved himself intelligent and enterprising as a diplomat.

2. This picture of a messenger delivering a letter to the king conveys a lively sense of urgency and excitement; it is probable that Chaucer's reports of his diplomatic activities would have been received with less eagerness at court. But the court circle consisted of a relatively small number of people. Men came into the king's presence with news, requests, problems of practical politics, and the court circle lived at the centre of activity. Chaucer's talents would be noticed; his successes remembered. He would no doubt have won a reputation for reliability and common-sense which would have recommended him to the king as a messenger who could be trusted. (BM Sloane 2433A f. 63ᵛ)

In 1372, Chaucer was sent to Italy to negotiate with the Genoese; his instructions were to arrange for a special seaport for the use of Genoese merchants. This visit to Italy, which included a call at Florence, must have excited and stimulated Chaucer. The great Italian writers, Petrarch and Boccaccio, each had a probable influence on his writing which will be discussed later, but perhaps it was the atmosphere of Italy itself, the contrasts it afforded with

England and France, the chance to see its art and its architecture
for himself, which would have coloured Chaucer's mental picture
of Italy and enlarged the scope of his imagination. This journey was
followed by others; Chaucer became an established member of the
king's diplomatic service.

3. Venice is shown as a crowded clutter of buildings on a waterfront. Its architecture even at this time suggests an Eastern influence, and the harbour is
crowded with shipping. Venice was a cosmopolitan city where merchants from
East and West met to trade, and where the powerful merchant classes had helped
to make the city rich and beautiful. Chaucer would also have found contrasts with
London in Genoa; it too, was a major port which brought together traders from
all over the known world. (Bodleian MS. Bodl. 264 f. 218^r)

Already he was beginning to write. *The Book of the Duchess* was written within a year or two of 1369, on the death of Blanche, the wife of John of Gaunt (Lionel's brother). John of Gaunt's grief was deep and sincere, and Chaucer and his own wife Philippa became close friends of the family of John of Gaunt. Yet the poem was probably not written purely out of affection and sympathy. Commemorative poems, addressed to the great and to important patrons, had been written since Classical times, and Chaucer was following an ancient tradition. His work had its reward, perhaps in that very association with John of Gaunt's household which was to follow. He and his wife were later given pensions of ten pounds by John for their services. So this poem of Chaucer's was written to please a patron, and perhaps in the hope of advancing himself in the world. That it had a practical as well as a literary purpose in no way diminishes its value: the idea that painting and poetry and music should be the work of creative artists who have no motive but an artistic one, is very modern. In Chaucer's day there was no such thing as 'art for art's sake'.

Chaucer had married his wife Philippa in about 1366; in 1367 Edward III granted her a pension of ten marks for her services as *domicella*, or handmaid, to the Queen,[4] and she continued to fulfill these duties and to serve in the household of John of Gaunt after her marriage. It was (we suppose) for his son, 'little Lewis' that Chaucer wrote his manual of astronomy, *Treatise on the Astrolabe*, but little trace survives of the rest of their family. There was almost certainly a son, Thomas, and a daughter, Elizabeth. In 1387, Philippa died; it is not impossible that Chaucer took another wife, but what we know of his family life is limited to these few hints of a marriage in which both partners were actively engaged in the service of the royal households, as their positions demanded.

The years between 1373 and 1376 were years of great success for Chaucer. He was given a house in London, on a lease which was to run for his lifetime; it was situated '*above the gate of Aldgate*'.[5] Among the appointments and awards showered on him was the important post of Controller of Customs and Subsidy in Wool and Hides. It was stipulated that he should carry out the work himself, and not delegate it, as was often done by such office-holders:

> Let the aforesaid Geoffrey keep his records in the said office with his own hand, and let him be continually present there; let him discharge all the duties of his office in his own person and not through a substitute.[6]

Later, while he was still in his thirties, he was again sent on missions abroad: to Flanders, to Paris, to Montreuil. (He was allowed, during these periods of absence, to delegate his work as Controller.) Even the death of Edward III in 1377 did not affect Chaucer's position or diminish his prosperity. His posts and positions were renewed in the name of the ten-year-old Richard II.

It was probably during the years 1381–7, while he was in England, that he wrote a number of his poems: *Troilus and Criseyde*, *The Parliament of Fowls*, *The Legend of Good Women* and the story of Palamon and Arcite, which was to become *The Knight's Tale*. He also translated Boethius' *The Consolation of Philosophy*, with a skill which shows he was a competent Latin scholar.

These are the works of a mature and successful man, writing for the enjoyment of his friends and patrons at court. It is probable that he had written a number of the stories which were later to be incorporated into *The Canterbury Tales;* he had made his mark as a man and as a writer, when in 1386 he began to lose influence and position because of strife at court. Even a man as successful as Chaucer had been throughout his life at court, was at the mercy of personal dislike and the power of court factions. His position was by no means secure.

Chaucer left London and the court circle, and retired to Kent. He had been made a Justice of the Peace there in 1385 and may already have been spending some of his time in the county, but now he gave up his house over Aldgate. He had got into debt. (There were several summonses to pay sent to him at this time.) He lost his wife, Philippa, in 1387. But his period of exile was not entirely clouded by gloom: in 1386 he was returned as a Member of Parliament for Kent.

In 1389, Richard II took a firmer grasp upon his kingship and exercised his right to choose his own ministers and officials: Chaucer was recalled from Kent to become Clerk of the King's Works, an office which gave him charge of the maintenance of the royal residences. The work was probably time-consuming and demanding, and it may have come at an inopportune moment because Chaucer was already working on *The Canterbury Tales*. He must have found it extremely difficult to continue in the intervals of an exacting administrative career. But the post gave him financial security and a position in the London world which he had lost a few years earlier: the second chance was presumably welcome, and the work on the *Tales* went on.

4. This drawing of London Bridge and Tower conveys an impression of crowded buildings and great density in the city of London. It is a characteristic of medieval drawings of architecture that they seem to show a jumble of buildings rather than separate shops and houses. Although medieval towns were not planned so as to give well-designed areas of space to their inhabitants, it is probable that there was a certain spaciousness within the city walls, in gardens and squares. But streets were narrow and houses were built where they were needed, so that this medieval artist's view of his city may not be so misleading. (BM MS. 16 f. ii)

Chaucer died in 1400, after receiving his royal pension for the last time in June. *The Canterbury Tales* were never completed.

[1]M. M. Crow and C. C. Olson (Ed.) *Chaucer Life Records* (O.U.P., 1966) p. 13 [2]*ibid.* p. 15 [3]*ibid.* p. 31 [4]*ibid.* p. 67 [5]*ibid.* p. 145 [6]*ibid.* p. 149.

2

Chaucer's London and His World

Chaucer had a Londoner's view of England; that is, he, like many Londoners today, would probably have thought of the rest of the country as provincial. He mentions Lincoln (*The Prioress's Tale*), Cambridge and Trumpington (*The Reeve's Tale*), Dunmowe in Essex (*The Wife of Bath's Tale*), Oxford (*The Clerk of Oxenford*) and its suburb Oseney (*The Miller's Tale*), and Bath (*The Wife of Bath*) among the few, and on the whole, brief references to English places in the *Tales*. His own travels chiefly took him further afield, to the Continent, although he would have visited certain parts of England on business and he knew Kent well. But his knowledge of his native land was probably very sketchy; there can have been no one living in his day who knew it well by modern standards. Travel, though far easier and more usual than it had been a few centuries earlier, was still made difficult by poor roads, the danger of attack and robbery on the journey, and sheer ignorance of the terrain of any but the most populous parts of the country, where merchant-routes and pilgrim-routes were well established. (The route to Canterbury was not the only one of these: pilgrims travelled to Glastonbury, Walsingham, Gloucester and elsewhere.)

The 14th century Gough Map tells us what at least one map-maker knew. The coastline of southern and eastern England is far more accurately represented than that of the rest of the country. The scattering of place names is much thicker in the south-east, where most of the best-known and most important places were situated. The rest of the country has a vaguely defined shape which only very roughly corresponds with the real shape of the British Isles.

Up to a point, the Londoners of Chaucer's time thought like the people of today; for most people, home ground is familiar and the rest of the world more or less indistinct. But Chaucer's contempories had little means of finding out more about the rest of their country; there were no reference books or road-maps, and travelling was slow and uncertain. So it is probable that Chaucer's London,

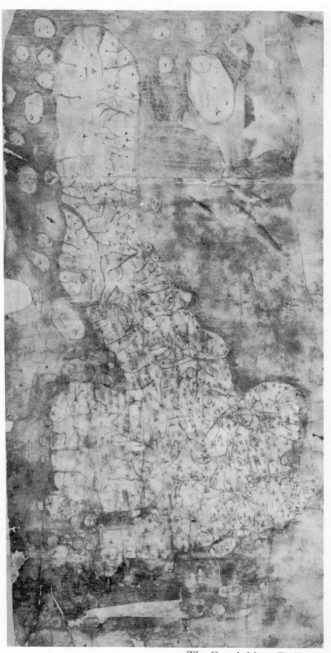

5. The Gough Map. (Bodleian)

together with Kent and some of the places he had visited on his missions for the king, made up his picture of the world, a picture in which London itself was very much in the foreground.

London has a place in the *Tales*. The Pardoner lived at Rouncival, a religious house in Westminster, which had a bad reputation for harbouring rascally pardoners. The Prioress spoke the French of Stratford-atte-Bowe, which then lay outside the city, but which has now become Stratford East. Many areas which are now well within Inner London were then outside the city walls, in the open countryside. But within the city itself were enclosed all the administrative offices with which Chaucer had to do; he would have met his friends there; he would have been at least on nodding terms with everyone of importance, because, comparatively speaking, the men of affairs who held important posts were few.

London probably contrasted as strongly with the other towns of England in Chaucer's day as the lives of the very rich contrasted with those of the very poor. William Dunbar, a Scottish 'Chaucerian' whom we shall meet in Chapter 10, describes London like this:

> *London, thou art of towns A per se,*
> *Sovereign of cities, most seemliest by sight,*
> *Of high renown, riches, and royalty,*
> *Of lords, barons, and many (a) goodly knight,*
> *Of most delectable lovely ladies bright,*
> *Of famous prelates in habits clerical,*
> *Of merchants of substance and might;*
> *London, thou art the flower of cities all.*[1]

Most towns had their fair share of dirt and rubbish, in the absence of any system of sanitation or refuse collection, but London's problems were larger because of its size:

> *The King to the mayor and sheriffs of the City of London: . . .*
> *whereas now, passing along the water of Thames we have beheld*
> *dung and laystalls and other filth accumulated in divers places*
> *and have also perceived the fumes and other abominable stenches*
> *arising therefrom, from the corruption which, if tolerated,*
> *great peril . . . will, it is feared, ensue.*[2]

We read of traffic accidents:

> *On Thursday . . . about the hour of vespers, two carters taking*
> *two empty carts out of the city were urging their horses apace,*
> *when the wheels of one of the carts collapsed . . . so that the*
> *cart fell on Agnes de Cicestre, who immediately died.*[3]

Street quarrels were common:

> *Copyn le Kyng and a certain William Osbern bargained for some . . . apples and wished to carry off five of them against the will of the bearer; thereupon he made a noise and clamour. There came a certain Thomas le Brewere, who reprimanded Copin and William for taking the apples against the wish of the vendor, so that angry words arose between them, and Copin and William assaulted Thomas le Brewere.*[4]

These scenes might perhaps have happened in other towns, but London far outstripped its rivals in size and importance. Those who had lived in towns had always enjoyed a degree of independence. Within their walls, the inhabitants had a small community—of perhaps three or four thousand people—which was in many respects self-sufficient. The countryside was never far away even in London; gardens and orchards were mingled with the houses, and outside the walls farmland stretched away.

Townsmen could be very exclusive; the gilds of merchants and artisans exercised a monopoly of the selling of their products. The only way into a gild was by means of apprenticeship, followed by a period of work as a journeyman. The workman who became a master and a member of his gild became a substantial and important member of the community. Chaucer's weaver, dyer, haberdasher, carpenter and tapestry-weaver are gildsmen with this tradition behind them.

6. In early 15th century shops the wares were few and personal service was the rule. (BM MS. Cot. Tib. A VII f. 93)

Apprentices were not always well treated:

> *Thomas and William Sewale, sons of Thomas Sewale of Canterbury, who had been apprenticed by their father to John Sharpe, came into court and complained that their master had been for a long time in Newgate and was unable to instruct them, and that his wife Margery had fed them insufficiently, had beaten them maliciously and had struck William on the left eye so violently that he lost the sight of that eye.*[5]

The system had glaring faults but standards of work and behaviour were maintained by the efforts of a small number of leading members of the gilds. Gilds were often ruthless in expelling unsatisfactory members and in preventing 'foreigners' (or strangers to the town) from carrying on their work there.

Little is known about the education available to the boys of a town in Chaucer's day, but there appears to have been an increase in literacy, and a number of ordinary men were sufficiently articulate to stand up for themselves in the law-courts, and to identify themselves with the Lollard movement for religious reform which will be discussed in Chapter 3; they made their voices felt in town and national affairs. We know that discipline in the schools was strict and that beatings were common, but that seems to have been the case in elementary schools in almost every age. *The Booklover* of Richard de Bury tells us that nevertheless:

> *Scholars as a class are commonly not well brought up, and unless they are held in check by the rules of their elders, are puffed up with all sorts of nonsense.*[6]

Standards of learning and teaching are difficult to determine. Richard de Bury says that

> *we ought to take much better care of a book than of a shoe. . . . There should be a natural decorum in the opening and closing of books. . . .*[6]

The point evidently needed making. Scant respect for books may have gone with incompetent teaching. There was evidently an increasing tendency for boys to be taught to construe their Latin lessons into English rather than into French during the 14th century. Trevisa explains that in the past boys learned to speak French as well as to understand Latin, by translating from one language into the other; now, he says:

*In all the grammar schools of England children leave the French
and construe and learn in English . . . now children of grammar
schools know no more French than their left heel, and that is
bad for them if they pass the sea and travel in strange lands.*[6]

Chaucer's was perhaps the last generation to gain a knowledge of
French with a grounding in Latin.

Town life in Chaucer's day had a distinctive character, a liveliness and fullness which would have attracted talented and ambit-

7. At this royal dinner those present sit at long tables, with a number of dishes on
the table before them. Each course consisted of not one, but a group of dishes.
There are no forks: forks were not to be introduced into England until two
centuries after Chaucer's death. Every man carried his own knife, with which he
cleaned his nails, cut up his food, and performed any other tasks for which it was
suitable. Some of the guests can be seen to be using their fingers to pick up the
morsels of food they want from the serving dishes. (BM MS. Royal 1 E ix f. 132ᵛ)

ious young men, to London in particular. There was scope in London for a man to make his fortune, or to follow a career in law, in the civil service or at court—even to become Lord Mayor, as the legendary Dick Whittington set out to do. There was no reason for anyone to restrict himself to a single career or profession; all the major professions shared their most promising recruits. Chaucer himself was, by turn, a diplomat, a civil servant, a courtier, a Member of Parliament, a soldier and a Justice of the Peace. Once his name was known, he was given opportunities to prove himself; success opened up further avenues. Chaucer was, in a sense, a public servant, and that meant that he could be required to carry out almost any kind of duty. London offered unique opportunities because it was the centre of government and administration. Chaucer seems to have been entirely at home among the bustle and appears to have revelled in the parade of varied human life which London brought before him.

FROM LONDON TO CANTERBURY

A number of early maps of the world show Jerusalem as its centre. Rome is frequently marked, too. Early medieval map-makers were usually monks, and they viewed Christendom as the central area of the earth, with the Holy City in the middle. It is doubtful whether pilgrims made much use of such maps. Actually travelling across Europe brought them into contact with the day to day realities of the journey: the problems of crossing the Alps and the sea, in particular. But there were maps drawn from a 'pilgrim' point of view, that is, they set Jerusalem in the centre of the world, and they show where Rome is situated. (The third centre of international pilgrimage was the shrine of St James at Compostella in Spain.) Such large-scale pilgrimages might take years to accomplish. But Chaucer's pilgrims travelled a well-tried route closer to home—the road which ran from London to Canterbury.

Parties of pilgrims usually set out from Southwark, as his company does, and it seems to have been customary to spend the first night at Dartford, although Chaucer himself does not mention Dartford. Chaucer is not anxious to match the length of the tales to the places which the pilgrims should have reached. He merely points out a place here and there as they pass through it, to keep up the illusion of travelling: '*Lo Depeford*', '*Lo Greenwich*'; '*Lo Rouchestre*'. The journey would have taken real pilgrims several

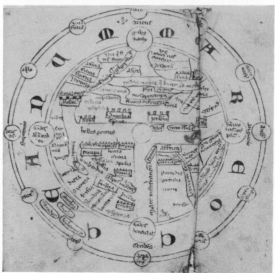

8. These two maps of the world show how schematic an impression the early mapmakers had. They are diagrams rather than maps. In the first, the ocean is shown running round the edge of a circular earth, and across its equatorial diameter. Above and below the zones of the earth pass progressively from hot, to temperate, to cold. In the second map, the circling ocean is marked again, with a T-shaped sea dividing the continents. The East is at the top of the map, with the Mediterranean Sea forming the stem of the T. Jerusalem is in the centre of Asia, near the coast. Rome lies in the centre of Europe, near the coast. The African continent is on the right. In this scheme of things the most important places in the world occupy the most important positions, and the world is seen to be symmetrical, the tidy creation of a God with a tidy mind. (Bodleian MS. D'Orville 77 f. 100/MS. e. Mus. 223 f. 185)

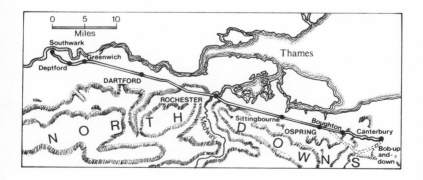

9. Lydgate and the Canterbury Pilgrims leave Canterbury. (BM MS. Royal 18D II f. 148) The map of the Pilgrim's Way shows all the places mentioned by the pilgrims on the journey. The places where they would probably have stopped for the night are in capital letters.

days, from one end of the old Roman road called Watling Street to the other.

Chaucer's pilgrims never arrive at Canterbury because *The Tales* were not completed, but their journey, as far as it goes, seems to be quite typical of the journeys of contemporary Canterbury pilgrims. Chaucer wanted his readers to recognize the pilgrimage's details, so as to give his plan for the stories a basis in common experience. The nearest modern parallel to such a prolonged and normally tedious journey is perhaps the crossing of the Continent by train. It is possible to fly round the world in less time than it took Chaucer's pilgrims to get from London to Canterbury.

[1]E. Rickert (Ed.) *Chaucer's World* (Columbia U.P., 1948) p. 3   [2]*ibid.* p. 11   [3]*ibid.* p. 13   [4]*ibid.* p. 15   [5]*ibid.* p. 107   [6]*ibid.* p. 119.

3

Chaucer: Politics and the Church

POLITICS

Chaucer was born into an England whose king still claimed a right to sit on the throne of France; gradually it was to become only too clear that such an ambition was no longer attainable. The relationship between England and France had been complicated since the Norman Conquest by the fact that for generations the English kings had held enormous estates in France. As land holders in France they were, in a sense, subjects of the French king, but in the late 12th century in the days of the Angevin Empire, their estates covered a greater area than those directly ruled by the king of France himself. The French king's sovereignty over such powerful subjects can have been no more than nominal. English presence on French soil became increasingly irksome to the French; English trade with Gascony drained French resources into England; the authority of English lords became intolerable to their French subjects: in 1337 a war began which was to last for a hundred years.

Edward III based his claim to the French throne upon the connection of his mother, Isabella, with the French royal house. (She was the sister of Charles IV.) He did not, however, assert this claim until 1340, three years after the fighting had begun, so it seems probable that his claim was merely an attempt to justify a war which was already under way.

At first England did well: the battle of Sluys in 1340; the battle of Crécy in 1346; the siege of Calais which ended in 1347—all were English victories. But the cost in men and resources was heavy, and the English did not make the best strategic use of the temporary advantages they gained. The period of English success was coming to an end when Chaucer was a child. Nevertheless, it had brought a certain prosperity to the English suppliers of food, clothing and arms for the armies, and Chaucer's family and friends must have enjoyed the security of living in a rich, powerful and successful country, whose prosperity had an apparent solidity.

The Black Death struck England in 1348. It was one of those major outbreaks of plague which occur every few centuries. Its last traces were still causing smaller outbreaks twenty years later. it has been very difficult for historians to assess the number of deaths, but the loss of manpower for the armies as well as for agricultural work and the manufacturing of goods must have weakened England considerably. Although they won a brilliant victory near Poitiers in 1356, when Edward's eldest son, the Black Prince, routed the French king's army and captured the king himself, the English had to make terms because they lacked the resources to follow up their victory. In 1360, at Brétigny, Edward abandoned his claim to the French throne, in return for the possession of Calais, Ponthieu and Aquitaine, together with the promise of three million crowns in ransom for the French king. Chaucer's part in the events of these years was small, but he was present at some of the negotiations.

10. This picture of a battle at the gates of a city achieves its impact by making buildings, tents and people jostle one another for space. The people are more important than their surroundings, so they are shown proportionately large, with no regard for perspective or realism. The anxious inhabitants of the town are seen looking out of their windows at the scene. Many of the techniques and tactics of late medieval warfare are shown here: two knights fight on horseback; there is hand-to-hand fighting; the enemy is camped outside the city, presumably to lay siege to it, but we are shown an actual battle in progress. A number of details of arms and armour are recognizable. The battles Chaucer saw must have been noisy and confused, as this battle evidently is. (BM Stowe 54 f. 83)

From this point English successes became fewer and more costly. The English armies continued to use the tactics which had won them their early battles; pitched battles and siege warfare had worked well in the first half of the century, but they were becoming out of date. The French avoided conflicts unless they were likely to be victorious.

The Black Prince became ill while he was campaigning in Spain and never fully recovered. A new king, Charles V, had replaced John on the throne of France and was considerably more able than his predecessor. Edward III was growing old. The raids of the English army no longer won them rich prizes, but merely angered the French and caused resentment and ill-feeling against English soldiers in France.

11. A walled city. (BM Add. 42130 f. 164ᵛ)

The English Parliament came to resent the frequent demands for money for campaigns. John of Gaunt, fourth son of Edward III, supported popular feeling directed against those powerful members of the higher clergy who were also officers of the Crown; they were widely blamed for squandering the people's money on a war which brought neither profit nor glory. In opposition to his brother, the Black Prince joined forces with Edmund Mortimer. (Edmund was married to Philippa, daughter of Chaucer's patron Lionel, Duke of Clarence, and his wife Elizabeth.) Chaucer's work therefore brought him into the midst of the political squabbles of his day.

The Black Prince's death in 1376 probably prevented the bitter disagreements from turning into open conflict between the parties of magnates.

Richard II succeeded his grandfather Edward III in 1377; he was the Black Prince's only son, a weak and gentle boy, who was to grow into an indecisive and unsatisfactory king, quite unable to govern the strong men who were his subjects. For several years the government was in the hands of a council of barons who found it difficult to agree amongst themselves, because they represented different factions. The war in France was going badly. In 1381 popular feeling found a small expression in the Peasants' Revolt. The revolt was soon put down, partly because it lacked cohesion and unified leadership. This was probably stimulated by the levy exacted in 1380, which extorted money the poor could not afford to pay, but also by a combination of causes—economic, political, social—as complex and as difficult to untangle as those which sparked off the French Revolution. The young king met the rebels in person and quieted them; they were promised pardons, and charters freeing them from their serfdom and the restrictions placed on them by feudal law. Trustfully, the rebels returned to their homes. The concessions were, for the most part, withheld. In fact, the revolt may even have slowed down the process by which the agricultural workers of England slowly became free, because the ruling classes were afraid to give much licence to their underlings. For a time restrictions were enforced more strictly still.

We have already seen Chaucer's fate during the time of Richard's weakness in government. In 1386 Richard was forced to dismiss his chief ministers; in 1387 Thomas, Duke of Gloucester, with the Earls of Arundel and Warwick, defeated the king on the battlefield; in 1388 a Parliament which earned the nickname of the 'Merciless Parliament' ordered the king's supporters to be exiled, imprisoned or executed. Chaucer was among those who suffered, even though his position was unimportant in comparison with the offices held by the powerful participants in the conflict.

Richard, as we know, reasserted himself, and Chaucer was given a new office. Richard tried to strengthen his position by making a marriage with Isabella, the seven-year-old daughter of Charles VI of France. He also attempted to cement an alliance with the Pope, and to strengthen England's hold over Ireland. His efforts were sufficiently successful for him to have Gloucester, Arundel and Warwick arrested, and in 1397 another Parliament ordered the king's opponents to be punished; it reversed the Acts of the

12. A royal marriage. John I of Portugal marries Philippa of Lancaster. In this late 15th century picture, the royal couple stand in conventional poses, their hands joined by the bishop who is marrying them. Their elaborately-dressed retinues should be contrasted with the courtiers who are shown in illustration 2. The wealth and sophistication of court life is much more evident in this picture. (BM MS. 63 Royal 14.E iv. f. 284)

'Merciless Parliament'. John of Gaunt's eldest son, Henry Boling-broke was exiled, and with Gloucester and Arundel dead, Richard perhaps felt more secure. The exile of Henry was, however, to bring about his downfall. Henry returned to claim, not only his own inheritance, which he was denied on the death of his father, but the crown of England as well. Richard failed to realize that his power depended on the support of the magnates whom he had offended, and Henry's invasion was successful. Richard gave himself up. Probably he believed that if he consented to allow Henry to claim his inheritance, and to make him 'hereditary steward' of England Henry would leave him his throne, as he had promised to do. But Richard was imprisoned and forced to abdicate.

13. The captured Richard II is delivered into the hands of the citizens of London. (BM Harley MS. 1319 f. 53b)

We have no means of knowing how Chaucer really felt about the change of king, although he wrote him a poem designed to bring himself to favourable notice called 'The Complaint of Chaucer to his Purse'. Perhaps more important is the fact that Henry's success showed up serious weaknesses in the security of both throne and government in England. His own death followed a year later, in 1400. But while the usurpation revealed weaknesses, it also revealed strengths. England's greatest strength lay in its administrative system, in the bureaucracy of which Chaucer himself was a member. It provided continuity and stability in the face of startling changes in the balance of power within the country. Justice was done and taxes were gathered; the daily life of the people was administered in a businesslike manner.

Chaucer's England was, then, not a peaceful or a stable place to live in; violence and the threat of war were always in the background; the rule of the barons, ever since the Norman Conquest, had been forceful and vigorous: a display of might. The ruling class was a class of professional soldiers. By contrast, the administrators constituted a comparatively stable bureacracy, with a system which had been slowly evolving to meet changing needs at least since the time of Henry I. Chaucer and his class served in royal and noble households, and they were given posts in the administration. The two worlds were not entirely separate, and Chaucer straddled both.

Many records of the work of the civil service, of diplomatic activities, of military life survive from Chaucer's day. A king's herald, in the 15th century, swore an oath of loyalty to his master, as Chaucer must have done:

> *First ye shall swear that ye shall be true to our high and excellent prince, our soverign lord that here is, and to him that makes you herald. And if ye have any knowledge or hear any imagination or treason, which God defend that ye should, but in case that ye do, ye shall discover it to his high grace or to his noble council.*[1]

We read of preparations of war, of '*the repair of habergeons, kettle hats, plates, basinets, jacks, doublets, worsted stuffs, targets, lances, arras, seats, streamers, standards, banners, chests.*'[2] Horses were bought for the baggage trains to carry all this equipment across France:

> *We will and command you to buy for our use two hundred horses for our carriage and baggage. And moreover we command you to pay for the charges and expenses of the keepers of these said horses, and for all manner of charges for the same horses until they are brought to us.*[3]

14. Blacksmiths were to be found in towns and villages in a society which made extensive use of the horse, as a beast of burden, as a vehicle in war and for travelling, and for sport. This 15th century woodcut shows the blacksmith's tools and equipment in some detail. (BM PB 1 Blacksmith)

Men had to be paid for the time they spent in the king's service, if they did not owe him their service as his knights:

> To Lawrence Chesse and William Wodeward seamen of Greenwich, by agreement with them made by certain lords of the King's Council for their wages and expenses and for those of 60 men at arms and 40 bowmen, to go with them in the King's service in a barge etc. . . £50.[4]

> To John Orewell, the King's sergeant at arms, sent to the town of Ghent by order of the King and his Council with letters of credence of the King to the good men of the said town, for his wages and expenses, and for hire of men and boats for his safe conduct, for fear of the King's enemies in Flanders . . . £17–10s.[5]

Here is an account of the campaign of 1359–60, at which Chaucer himself was present.

> The King arrived at Calais on Monday next before All Saints [Nov. 1], where he remained eight days. He divided his army into three [columns]: one he kept with himself; another column he gave to his eldest son, the Prince of Wales [that is, Edward, the Black Prince]; the third column he intended for the Duke of Lancaster. . . . The three columns marched by different routes. . . and . . . formed a junction before Rheims, lying all around the city in hamlets for a month at Christmastime . . . . Lords and Knights of the King's column made a raid from Rheims nearly to Paris. They ambushed themselves and sent their scouts up to the gates of the city. They made such an uproar in the suburbs that those within the city had not the courage to come forth . . . . The King of England afterwards broke up from before Rheims and marched towards Chalons. . . . Five English esquires . . . having only one coat of mail and three archers, were in a cornmill near Regentz, a fortress held by the English not far from Auxerre. Fifty men-at-arms, the troup and pennon of the Lord of Hanget, came to attack them; but the five defeated the fifty, taking eleven prisoners.[6]

THE CHURCH

Chaucer's society was coloured by religious beliefs, habits, customs, and rules to a degree which it is often difficult for us to realize. No one could live a life untouched by religion. Regular attendance at church was expected of everyone, even if there were some defaulters. Alice Palmer forgave William Chester, a baker, the debt he owed her when she died in 1456, on condition:

> That he from hence forward duly and continually keep and come to his church, and there abide and hear service as other good and faithful men of the same church.[7]

In business the Church's calendar of saints' days and feasts was often used to date transactions, for example, 'On the day after Michaelmas'; the terms of the Inns of Court and of the Universities of Oxford and Cambridge are still named after the Church's seasons: Michaelmas, Hilary, Easter, Trinity, and so on. The Church's seal was set upon a man at every major event in his life: at baptism, confirmation, marriage, and death; if he was devout he would go regularly to Mass, make regular confession to his priest and perform the penance for his sins which the priest prescribed. Even the less devout had a certain almost superstitious reverence for the trappings of religion.

There was a general respect for the holy remains of the saints. Such relics were believed to have power to cure the sick, to grant wishes, to make an oath more binding. Those who could afford them might even have relics of their own. Edward III owned 'A crystal vessel enclosed after the fashion of the Temple, partly of gold and ornamented with diverse gems, in which are relics.'[8]

Others revered the relics kept in certain churches in the shrines of the saints. It was to see such relics that pilgrims undertook their long and hazardous journeys. Richard Poynings, knight, left his precious relic to his wife on his death: 'I bequeath to my beloved wife . . . a cross containing a large piece of the Holy Cross.'[9] Each of his children was to have a piece too, but his wife was to keep the larger part, and when she died, this portion was to go to the Church of Stokecours, to be kept there forever. In such ways did churches come by their relics, not all of which can have been genuine.

On the payment of a fee, or in return for a gift to a monastery, Masses and prayers were said for the souls of the dead:

> I will that . . . a priest be found two years to sing the great trental of St Gregory for our souls especially and for my lady my mother and for Sir John, Lord of Arundel and of Malt-revers. . . .[10]

Thus Sir Richard Poynings tried to provide for his own soul and for that of his wife in 1428. The Church's hold did not relax with death; those who offended the Church risked excommunication, which cut a man off from all the sacraments of the Church, denied him Christian burial, and consigned him to hell if he died before the ban was removed:

> *We excommunicate, damn, anathematize, and exclude from the threshold of the Holy Mother Church: those who disturb the peace of the realm, those who flout the laws . . . or steal the goods of the church . . . all usurers, incendiaries zealous in evil; those who have knowingly and wittingly sworn falsely by those things most sacred; those who commit sacrilege. . . .*
> *May they be accursed withindoors and withoutdoors, going in and coming out, eating, drinking, sleeping, waking, standing, sitting, walking, talking . . . . As these lamps are extinguished, so may their souls be extinguished in hell with the devil and his angels—unless they repent and come to make worthy penance and restitution.[11]*

The law-abiding paid their tithes (or dues to the Church of one tenth) with greater or lesser scrupulousness:

> *We will that a tenth part of the crops, not after expenses have been paid, but of the whole amount without any deduction, be counted.[12]*

In these and a myriad other ways the people of the Middle Ages lived their lives in close relation to the Church.

In more populous parts of the country a variety of members of the clergy were commonly to be seen. The prince of the ecclesiastical hierarchy was, of course, the Pope; below him in rank, archbishops, bishops and abbots wielded great power over the lives of ordinary people who lived on the lands which lay under their jurisdiction. A bishop or an abbot was in a sense a baron, because he controlled areas of land whose inhabitants were his serfs and villeins, just as if they belonged to a knightly lord. He also had the care or *cure* of their souls. A good bishop set an example to clergy and laity alike by giving alms, showing hospitality, living a holy life. But there were many ambitious men who saw a bishopric as a post which gave prestige and power in the world; such men collected rich gifts from a royal patron in the form of 'livings' and 'prebends'; these were church posts which carried a good income. The holder of a number of these offices, especially if he was also a bishop, could not hope to carry out his duties adequately, but he could draw on the incomes which came his way and live well at court.

Chaucer does not give us a bishop in *The Canterbury Tales*, or an abbot (his counterpart at the head of a large and wealthy monastery), but he does describe a worldly monk and a ladylike prioress. Not every man or woman who entered a religious order in the Middle Ages did so out of straightforward desire to live the life of a monk or nun. A number of children were given to monasteries by their parents in infancy, or at the age of seven when they were believed to have attained the age of reason. Women were consigned to convents against their will, particularly those for whom no husbands could be found.

Whether the community was subject to the fundamental Rule of St Benedict, or to one of the rules drawn up to govern the lives of members of one of the later orders, such as the Cistercians, the rule laid down the proper procedure for living every hour of the day and every day of the year, for maintaining proper 'custody' of every part of the body, every thought, every word. The religious gave up all claim to the right of independent action or freedom of decision, in return for a discipline which, it was believed, was the best possible means of chastening the self-centred soul into holiness.

The strain of living strictly according to the monastic rule was considerable, as it is today. It is not surprising that those with no vocation to the life broke the rules. A member of a religious order took a threefold vow: of poverty, chastity, and obedience. Chaucer's Monk breaks all these vows with a joyful boldness which leads Chaucer to remark that he is '*A manly man, to have been an abbot able*', a man of vigour who might rise to the position of a worldly abbot. He is fond of hunting *('that lovede venerie')* and fine clothes:

> *I seigh his sleves purfiled at the hond*
> *with grys, and that the fyneste of a lond;*
> *and, for to festne his hood under his chyn,*
> *He hadde of gold ywroght a ful curious pyn;*
> *A love-knotte in the gretter ende ther was.*

He is fat, well-dressed, confident, mounted upon an excellent horse. He sees no reason why he should pore over books:

> *What sholde he studie and make hymselven wood,*
> *upon a book in cloystre alwey to poure,*

or work with his hands at humble tasks, as St Augustine instructs. There are numerous examples of equally worldly figures among the abbots. In an early version of the 'Jackdaw of Rheims' story, an abbot of Corvey wears gold rings *'according to the showy custom of such wealthy abbots, among other pieces of worldly show'*.

The friars had won themselves a more doubtful reputation than the monks. When St Francis and St Dominic had brought together their bands of wandering religious, the medicants, in the early 13th century, they had had a very different vision. The friars were to travel in absolute poverty, depending on those they served, or those to whom they preached, to give them food and shelter. They were to live as Christ's apostles had done. But the wandering life appealed to men who would not commit themselves to a cloister, and all sorts of ruffians called themselves friars. A 14th century satirical poem mocks friars:

> *And fatter men about the ears*
> *Saw I never than are these friars. . . .*
> *They deal with purses, pins and knives,*
> *with girdles, gloves for maid and wives. . . .*[13]

Chaucer's Friar, too, is little better than a wandering pedlar: he carries small items to tempt the ladies:

> *His typet was ay farsed ful of knyves*
> *and pynnes, for to yeven faire wyves.*

He sings and dallies with the women he meets; he is *'wantowne'* and *'merye'*. So plausible is his tongue that *'He was the beste beggere in his house'*; he is the best beggar in his house.

It often fell to the parson to take the services of the local parish, to care for the people who lived there, and to carry out the small duties neglected by the higher clergy. Chaucer's *'povre Persoun'*, the poor parson, has no wealth, but much holiness; he is learned and conscientious in preaching the gospel; he gives generously of his slender resources to help the needy. Chaucer brings him in in sharp contrast to his other clergy, with their glaring vices. There were, of course, good men as well as bad among the medley of clerks, priests, deacons, acolytes, scholars, clergy in every kind of holy orders (and there were many). We shall meet Chaucer's Summoner, Pardoner and Clerk later. Chaucer's picture of the churchmen of his day deliberately throws the abuses into relief because fallible human beings are immediately entertaining, and a catalogue of the virtues of truly holy men would make the *General Prologue* dull reading. Chaucer's sketch of the Church and clergy he knew is, in a sense, a caricature rather that a realistic portrait; curious and amusing features are exaggerated. Yet the sheer number and variety of the clergy he introduces, in proportion to the whole number of his pilgrims, shows how large a part the clergy played in ordinary social life in the 14th century.

Popular religion often made little distinction between folklore, superstition and the real teachings of the Church. Ordinary people were not trained in doctrinal studies; many must barely have understood the Christian faith they professed. Gilbert of Nogent, who lived at the turn of the 11th century, describes how country people made a saint of an ordinary boy:

> *I have indeed seen, and blush to relate, how a common boy nearly related to a certain most renowned abbot, and squire (it was said) to some knight, died in a village hard by Beauvais on Good Friday, two days before Easter. Then, for the sake of that sacred day whereon he had died, men began to impute a gratuitous sanctity to the dead boy. When this had been rumoured among the country-folk, all agape for something new, then forthwith oblations and waxen tapers were brought to his tomb by the villagers of all that country around.*[14]

We are told how a woman kept a piece of communion bread in her mouth instead of swallowing it, and then placed it in one of her beehives. The bees, *'recognising the might of their Creator, built . . . a tiny chapel of marvellous workmanship. Wherein they set up an altar of the same material and laid thereon this most Holy Body'.*[15] When the woman saw what they had done, she went at once and confessed her sin to the priest.

Berthold Von Regensburg in the 13th century told this story: a group of travellers were drinking at an inn, and joking among themselves when they were joined by a stranger. One of them said in jest that if anyone would buy his soul, he should have it cheaply, and they would all drink to the bargain. The stranger paid the price asked and, at the end of a merry evening, snatched him up before their eyes and carried him off to hell; he was, of course, the Devil. Such tales must have been told and enjoyed by ordinary people, even those who could not understand the services they heard in Latin at Church.

Popular piety looked for means of expression which were open to the laity. Devotion to the Virgin Mary became increasingly popular, partly because she was a figure towards whom the simplest could feel a warm affection. Devotional 'gilds' were set up, bound together by a common devotion to Mary:

*In worship of Jesus Christ and of His Dear Mother, Saint
Mary, and in the holy fellowship of heaven, and especially of
Our Lady Saint Mary of the Assumption, this fraternity is
begun in the town of Wiggenhall for the worship of Our Lady.*[16]

Other gilds were devoted to St Christopher, or to the saying of
the Lord's Prayer (the Paternoster gilds). Many of the laity confessed their sins, did penance, and strove to meet the standards of
personal virtue demanded of them.

But there were those who questioned the influence of the organ-
ized Church. In 1390 we hear of a penance imposed upon those
who had failed to bring straw for the archbishop's horse:

*Ignorance, the mother of error, so much hath blinded and
deceived certain persons, to wit, Hugh Pennie, John Forstall,
John Boy, John Wanderton, William Hayward, and John
White . . . that they, against the coming of (the) archbishop
to his palace of Canterbury on Palm Sunday eve . . . . being
warned by the bailiff to convey and carry that, straw and other
litter to the aforesaid Palace . . . refused and disdained to do
their due services.*[17]

The penitents were ordered to go bareheaded at the front of the
archbishop's procession carrying on their shoulders bags stuffed
with hay and open at the mouth to show their contents. They
were thus publicly humiliated. Such practices led the more articulate and better educated among the middle classes to question
whether the Church deserved the respect it demanded.

Open abuses were comparatively common among the clergy in
the 14th century and the well-fed, richly-clothed cleric, the monk
who had forgotten his vow of poverty, chastity and obedience, the
prioress whose refinement has little monastic simplicity about it,
the poor parish priest, on whose (often ignorant) head fell all the
business of pastoral care which his superiors neglected, all these
and their like are the targets of Chaucer's ironic pen. It is not
difficult to imagine the resentments which the laity felt towards
these privileged members of the ecclesiastical hierarchy.

Chaucer's Host '*smells a Lollard in the wind*', when the poor Parson
protests against swearing. The Lollards were followers of John
Wycliffe who accused the Church of corruption and questioned
its teaching. He translated the Bible into the language of the common
people, so as to make the scriptures available to those who were
not professional clergy. Unrest bred the demand for reform, and
Wycliffe and his followers put into words what others had long felt.

As more and more members of the middle classes learned to read, they came to be better informed on a number of matters which they had hitherto been content to leave to those they accepted as their betters. Articulate, industrious, ambitious men beheld some of the more obvious abuses practised by the clergy with perhaps a certain envy of the ease with which they got their wealth; certainly with little respect for the privileges of the clergy. Equally, it is not surprising that they were unwilling to give that unquestioning obedience to the Church's authority which the Church had been accustomed to expect from the laity. It was among such men that Lollardy gained a foothold. Lollard members of the artisan class, and priests from the lower middle classes (such as Chaucer's poor Parson—if he was indeed a Lollard) were hounded more fiercely in the reign of Henry IV than they had been in Richard II's day. Henry could only attempt to root out Lollardy from its seat in the University of Oxford and try to frighten off fresh supporters by imposing by law the traditional penalty for heresy—burning at the stake. Influential men, men of rank, were still faithful to the movement and it also continued to flourish underground among the section of society to which poor craftsmen belonged.

The Lollard movement, then, had economic and social apects which enabled it to keep its foothold among the members of certain social classes. It was not only a religious movement, but a movement of self-expression, a symptom of a new independence of thought and judgment among the middle classes. Its religious aspects included straightforward disgust at the abuses practised by the Church, and at Oxford, much deeper questionings of the Church's standpoint on such doctrines as that of transubstantiation and free will. Wycliffe's translation of the Bible into the vernacular made those who were able to obtain a copy much better equipped to argue the case for their views against the clergy who quoted Scripture in support of the Church's actions. John of Gaunt's sympathies for the cause may have rubbed off on Chaucer.

In 1407 William Thorpe was examined before Archbishop Arundel because he had objected to pilgrimages which were undertaken in a holiday spirit and without real piety:

> *What sayest thou to the third point that is certified against thee, preaching openly in Shrewsbury that 'pilgrimage is not lawful'?*[18]

William Thorpe's offence was that he had attacked an institution which had become very lucrative to the Church, and which was so much a commonplace in England that it was as natural for Chaucer to choose to set his *Canterbury Tales* in the context of a group pilgrimage as it might be for a modern writer to put a collection of short stories in the mouths of a group of people on a package coach tour.

PILGRIMAGES

Pilgrimages had first become popular in the 11th century, when large parties travelled to the Holy Land. The Crusades (which were in a sense pilgrimages in their own right) opened up the routes to the East, and offered some protection to the traveller at least in those areas which were held by the Christians at various times during the 12th century, so that pilgrimages to the Holy Land became increasingly common. Pilgrimages to the shrine of St James at Compostella in Spain and to Rome were also popular, but for those with less time to spare, or smaller resources, local pilgrimages to the shrines of saints in their home country must have offered something of the same excitement and satisfaction. A medieval pilgrimage was more than a religious act: it was a holiday, and an opportunity to travel which probably came to few men in their lifetimes. Chaucer, the seasoned traveller, is very much an exception. The poor spent the greater part of their lives in or near the village where they were born. So Chaucer's Canterbury pilgrims were engaged in an expedition which they would expect to find pleasurable and amusing, as well as edifying.

15. In the early 14th century, a much more simply-drawn picture than 26 shows a traveller with a staff (BM MS. Royal 10 E. iv. f. 114ᵛ)

Apart from the tomb of St Thomas à Becket at Canterbury, the tomb of the murdered Edward II at Gloucester Cathedral and the shrine of Our Lady at Walsingham were popular resorts of pilgrims, and the monks who were fortunate enough to possess such a shrine earned great wealth for building and other purposes from the gifts of the pious.

16. This drawing of the murder of Thomas à Becket was made about 1200, not long after the event. The picture emphasises the fact that Becket was murdered in a place of sanctuary; it was this breach of the Church's right to protect anyone who came to the altar for safety which caused the furore over the Archbishop's death, rather than the murder itself. Becket's death in a holy place gave him an aura of martyrdom and he was soon canonized. (BM MS. Harley 5102 f. 32)

Becket's claim to sainthood rested chiefly on his 'martyrdom'. For years he stood out obstinately against the attempts of Henry II to bring certain of the Church's legal prerogatives under the control of the Crown. When he was murdered in Canterbury Cathedral, the killing constituted a breach of the law of sanctuary by which anyone taking refuge at the altar was protected. Feeling ran high against the king who was believed to have given orders to the murderers. Henry went in penitence through the streets and allowed himself to be publicly whipped to show his repentance; he saved his own reputation but already miracles were being reported, and Becket's tomb soon became a shrine. The cult of St Thomas caught on, as such cults often did, but for some reason, the Canterbury pilgrimage became established as one of the most valuable, and its popularity did not fade.

17. The travellers entering this inn, and sitting down to eat at a common table, come from all levels of society, and include clergy and women. The picture was executed early in the 15th century, but it shows that Chaucer's pilgrims at the end of the 14th century probably represented a fairly typical selection of the kinds of people who might travel together on pilgrimage. (BM Cot. Tib. A VII f. 90)

The merit of pilgrimage could be had by sending another man on pilgrimage as a proxy:

> *I bequeath to one man going for my soul as far as Jerusalem, 5 marks*

> *I bequeath 20 marks to hire one chaplain to go on pilgrimage to Rome.*[19]

Gilds were founded to help pilgrims: a gild at Boston in Lincolnshire provided a priest to say Mass *'very early and very late'* so that pilgrims should not endanger their piety by failing to hear Mass on their journey. Other gilds provided hostels for poor pilgrims, who could not afford to stay at inns as Chaucer's pilgrims did.

Pilgrimage was, in a sense, a very lucrative industry from which very material profits were made (apart from the spiritual benefits which the pilgrims gained.) The magnificence of the tomb of St Thomas as it is described by an early 16th century pilgrim shows the degree of wealth and importance which the more important shrines enjoyed:

> *But the magnificence of the tomb of St Thomas the Martyr, archbishop of Canterbury, is that which surpasses all belief. This, notwithstanding its great size, is entirely covered over with plates of pure gold; but the gold is scarcely visible from the variety of precious stones with which it is studded.*[20]

[1]E. Rickert *Chaucer's World* (Columbia U.P., 1948) p. 137–8   [2]*ibid* p. 288   [3]*ibid*. p. 288   [4]*ibid*. p. 290   [5]*ibid*. p. 290   [6]*ibid*. p. 294–5   [7]*ibid*. p. 388   [8]*ibid*. p. 390   [9]*ibid*. p. 389   [10]*ibid*. p. 396   [11]*ibid*. p. 393–4   [12]*ibid*. p. 388   [13]*ibid*. p. 375   [14]C. G. Coulton *Life in the Middle ages* (C.U.P., 1967) p. 16–7   [15]*ibid*. p. 71   [16]E. Rickert *Chaucer's World* (Columbia U.P., 1948) p. 397   [17]*ibid*. p. 392   [18]*ibid*. p. 264   [19]*ibid*. p. 267   [20]*ibid*. p. 370.

4

The Chaucer Universe

An educated man, living in the 20th century, has a picture of the universe based on what he has learned of astronomy and physics. He may have observed the sky for himself, but he is unlikely to have come to any conclusions which contradict the accepted notions, that the earth is spherical, that it circles the sun, that the sun is one star among many. The Flat-Earth Association has few members. He is probably sophisticated enough to separate this scheme of things from that in which he places his ideas of heaven and hell; the spiritual and the physical worlds exist for him on separate planes.

The medieval observer of the universe began from a quite different set of assumptions. Modern science, with its techniques of experimental verification of theories, was unknown to him. He would have learned that the earth was flat, that it was the centre of the universe, and that heaven and hell occupied a place in the same scheme of things as the earth itself. His personal observation would probably have confirmed what he had been taught: to the observer on the ground, the earth does appear to be flat and the sun, moon and stars appear to move across the dome of the sky as if they travelled round the earth. Most important is the fact that the medieval mind tended to accept that everything occupied the same level of reality: crops were to be planted in the proper season, unbaptized children would not go to heaven, certain magic spells cured warts, anyone unwise enough to sail out across the sea which surrounded the world would eventually fall from the edge. That is not to say that medieval thinkers were any more credulous than their modern counterparts; a large proportion of what we know consists of information which has come to us second-hand, and which we rarely bother to check for ourselves, but because of the shortage of works of reference and the immensely greater practical difficulties, medieval methods of checking were far less comprehensive than ours.

The idea of order was fundamental to medieval thought. Heaven and earth, Church and State were arranged in hierarchies which ranged all creation in a series of unalterable ranks. The notion of hierarchy pervaded society just as it did religious belief in the Middle Ages. The feudal system had undergone considerable changes and modifications since the time of the Conquest, but the majority of men still lived the lives of agricultural workers on the estates of great lords, and most of these men were still not free at the beginning of the 14th century. That is, they were in a sense their lord's property. But it became increasingly difficult and onerous for the landowners to exact all the dues in labour and in produce which were owed to them, and by the end of the century, when Chaucer died, there was a substantial body of prosperous peasants who were tenant farmers with some degree of independence. The upper levels of the peasantry probably merged into the lower levels of the country gentry and this rural middle class came to be known as the 'yeomanry'. Men with talent might win their way into the service of a great lord, and their material rewards could include the gift of lands or pensions. In such a way a family might better itself generation by generation, (as did the Paston family whose letters survive from the 15th century).

Within the Church, the Pope, archbishops, bishops, priests, and deacons in succession exercised authority over the laity. In the State, king, baron and knight dominated the lives of the common people. Within the hierarchy, or orders, of creation, God was defined as the uncreated, immortal, reasonable, animated, sensitive, being. He created the angels, who were immortal, reasonable, animated, sensitive; man, who was mortal, animated, sensitive, reasonable; animals, who were mortal, animated, sensitive; plants, which were mortal and sensitive; and inanimate objects, which merely existed. In heaven itself the angels were ranged in hierarchies after a scheme worked out by Pseudo-Dionysius: Alan of Lille preached a sermon at the end of the 12th century in which he taught that the man who imitates the angels in this life will be raised to the order most appropriate to his efforts in the next life:

> *Strive, then, O man, that you may be accredited with the fervour of love of the Order of Seraphim, or accounted to possess the fullness of knowledge of the Cherubim, or deserve to have the rational powers of judgement of the Order of Thrones, or, showing proper obedience, you may be companied with the Dominions, or, by ruling your subjects well, be a prince with the Principalities, or, resisting the Devil, you may be glorified with the Order of Powers, or, by performing miracles in*

chastising the flesh, you may be set in the Order of the Virtues,
or counted among the Archangels in teaching the more ex-
perienced, or that you may find a place among the angels in
preaching to the simple.[1]

The Italian poet Dante made use of the theory of the hierarchy
of heaven, as well as the picture of a hierarchy of hell and of purga-
tory, in his long poem, *The Divine Comedy*. There the poet is
escorted by his guide, Virgil, through the levels of hell, and by
the glorified figure of Beatrice, the lady he had loved in real life,
through the levels of heaven and meets in turn those who dwell
on each plane. Diagram 18 shows Dante's version of the medieval
notion of the hierarchy of heaven and hell. Numerous variations
of this belief were expressed by other writers, but the central idea
is common to them all: the universe is arranged in a fixed and
unalterable order of rank.

The arrangements of the social hierarchy were not of course
deliberately modelled on this philosophical theory: they were
determined during the course of centuries by the practical demands
of real life, and by a series of social, economic and political changes.
But when people looked at their society and tried to find reasons for
its structure, they had in their minds the notion of hierarchy which
was familiar to every scholar. They expected to find the members
of society ranked in a proper and necessary order. Most people in
the West today take it for granted that all human beings should
be considered equal before the law, and should have equal rights
and privileges in their society. We are heirs to a different philosophical tradition, which developed at the end of the 18th century,
through such writers as Rousseau; their views, in a modified form,
have become as much a natural background to our thought as the
medieval notion of hierarchy was to the people of Chaucer's day.

Wherever he turned, the educated man found this hierarchical
view of the universe endorsed by scholars. A complex system of
Biblical interpretation had evolved, in which the figures and events
of the Old Testament were shown to prefigure the coming of
Christ, and every text had its significance. Scripture could be
interpreted on three or four levels; it had a moral and an allegorical
sense as well as a literal one. Every number in Scripture and in
philosophy had a meaning: three for the Trinity; four for the four
evangelists, the seasons and the elements; seven for the vices and
the virtues; twelve for the apostles, the tribes of Israel and the
months of the year. Patterns and repeating motifs characterized

D

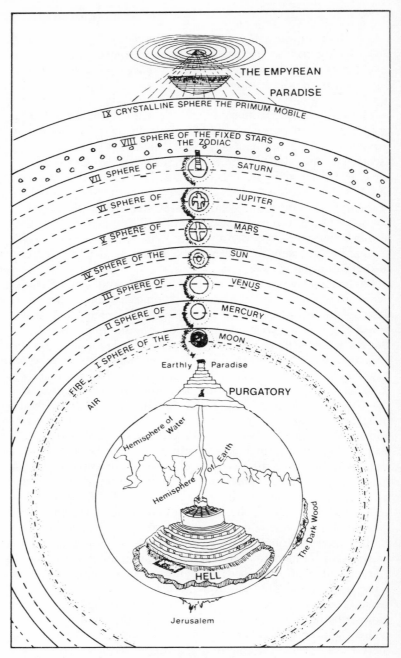

18. Dante's vision of the universe in the 'Divine Comedy'.

every attempt to explain the universe and to understand its shape
and its nature. The traditional song: 'Green Grow the Rushes-O'!
preserves some of the symbolism of numbers.

In man himself could be found a miniature universe, a microcosm,
where the macrocosm, or great cosmos, was reflected. There
reason ruled the senses, conscience governed the desire to sin, and
just as in an earthly kingdom and in heaven itself, there were
rebellions, so, in the individual, vice and virtue were seen as being
constantly at war, as in this confession:

> *I continued in the foul sin of drunkenness unto my last end, of*
> *an evil custom. Nevertheless, it was not my will, for greatly it*
> *displeased me and I sorrowed greatly that I could not leave*
> *that vice.*[2]

Behind these attitudes to the universe was the thinking of the
scholars of many centuries. They had tried to show how apparent
contradictions could be reconciled, anomalies in the texts explained
away, and the universe shown to be an integrated whole, designed
by God with concern for its beauty and unity. St Anselm, Archbishop of Canterbury at the end of the 11th century, remarked on
the *'beauty of reasonableness'*; he could not conceive of a God who
could fashion an untidy universe, or one which did not satisfy the
demands of human reason for system and order. On more than one
occasion he explains to his pupils that the contradictions they
think they have found can be explained away if only they will look
more carefully at the words they have used.

This underlying unity was envisaged as a kind of essential
harmony. Medieval thinkers often say that something is 'fitting' or
'appropriate', that it harmonizes or fits in with the general trend
of their arguments; they seem to have found that as convincing a
way of making out a case, as proving by logic alone that their
proposed conclusion is the only one which is possible.

The idea of harmony in music was an aspect of the general
notion of the harmony of the universe. Sounds were thought to
harmonize only if their mathematical relationships were exact;
the study of musical theory amounted to something very close to
arithmetic. It was possible to calculate the notes which the heavenly
bodies would make as they revolved in the heavens, by measuring
their distances from each other; they were thought to sing as they
travelled, and to give out a 'music of the spheres'.

The greatest difficulty which scholars encountered in their
attempts to discover the underlying unity of the scheme of things

19. In this Moralized Bible the astronomers and dialecticians are shown practising their skills; the dialecticians in particular seem to be engaged in fierce arguments. But the commentary reassures the faithful Christian that those whose learning seeks only vainglory and a reputation for cleverness among men will be overthrown in the end. (Bodleian MS. Bodl. 270^b f. 11^v)

was the discrepancy between the teaching of Scripture and that of the writers of the Classical works which survived into the Middle Ages. It is especially those works which dealt with cosmology, astronomy, astrology and medicine, which concern us here. Among the scientific writings which had come down from Classical times

20. This portrayal of Socrates and Plato, the Greek philosopher and his pupil, comes from a fortune-telling book of the 13th century. These ancient authorities give weight and importance to the work. A medieval reader would have found nothing out of place in the artist's portrayal of his philosophers in medieval dress. 'Socrates' holds a knife in his left hand with which he would from time to time trim the quill pen in his right. (Bodleian MS. Ashmole 304 f. 31^v)

were Plato's *Timaeus*, Boethius' work, *On Arithmetic* (which passed on a good deal of Pythagorean theory), and Macrobius' *Commentary on the Dream of Scipio*. These works of Classical writers were known in the 12th century, and they made it possible for the masters of the Cathedral School at Chartres, such as Thierry of Chartres, Bernard of Tours, William of Conches, to construct complex cosmologies in which Classical and Christian ideas were interfused. Thierry, for example, showed how the God the Trinity created the world by means of four kinds of causation:

> *God the Father is the efficient cause, the Son is the formal cause, the Holy Spirit is the final cause and matter the material cause.*[3]

He borrows from Plato the idea that the final cause of all creation is the World Soul, which he identifies with the Holy Spirit. From Pythagoras, whom he knew of through Boethius, he drew the idea that one is the only unchangeable and stable number, that unity therefore represents God, and all others numbers the perishable creation. Bernard Silvestris describes the Platonic notion of the Good, the Word and the World Soul, and makes it correspond with the Father, the Son and the Holy Spirit. From the Good comes the Word, which is understanding, and which contains the ideas of all things. The World Soul then makes the ideas concrete by giving them existence in the physical world. William of Conches wrote a commentary on the *Timeaus*, and in early manuscripts of his works are to be found diagrams of the world and the universe in which the familiar medieval schemata appear. Macrobius' work comments at length upon a fragment of Cicero, *The Dream of Scipio*, in which the hero is carried up above the earth in a vision, and the nature and shape of the universe is explained to him. In Cicero's work, the emphasis is upon the political and civil rules by which the world should be run; in Macrobius' commentary, a cosmology emerges which had an immense appeal to medieval thinkers looking for extensions of their theory and additional details to add to their scheme of things. Chaucer probably based his classifications of dreams in the first twenty lines of *The House of Fame* on Macrobius' dream-theory.

To this basis of elementary theories about the universe the following centuries added material in the form of works of Aristotle unknown to the early Middle Ages. These texts reached the West through the Arabs, who had translated them from the original Greek; Arabic philosophers had added commentaries of their own,

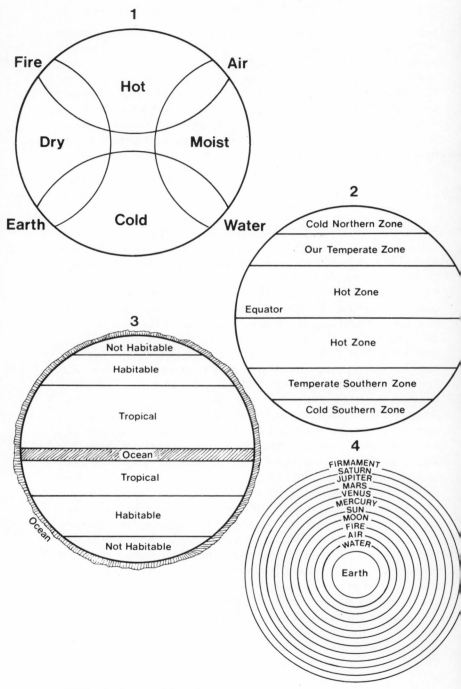

21. Medieval schemes of the universe.

so that the Aristotle that was studied in the West came to be strongly influenced by Arabic thought. It was in the fields of astronomy and astrology in particular that the Arabs made their contribution.

The two fields are difficult to separate in medieval thought; the signs of the Zodiac appear upon astrolabes, the instruments used for calculating the position of the heavenly bodies. Chaucer wrote a handbook, a *Treatise on the Astrolabe*, for little Lewis, on the method of using this complicated instrument. The Zodiac signs were not viewed merely as groups of stars; their astrological

22. The Sloane Astrolabe *c.* 1280. The astrolabe was an instrument of calculation; it enabled the astrologer/astronomer to work out when and where the planets could be expected to rise. It is marked out in a series of scales in such a way that when the inner ring is revolved the juxtaposition of signs and figures changes. Three-dimensional astrolabes later made more complex calculations possible; spherical instruments in the Science Museum in London date from later centuries. (BM 21)

significance was believed to be profound. A man's life was closely governed by the combination of heavenly bodies which presided over his birth. Above all, his temperament and constitution were determined by his time of birth. The superstition is far from dead in our own day. Most newspapers and magazines carry regular horoscopes.

The heavens form a great sphere to the observer on earth; the sun appears to run in an orbit around that sphere, and the stars and planets lie in a band on either side of the sun's path. In the course of the year, as the earth travels round the sun, the visible parts of the heavens change, and to an observer it seems that different groups of stars and planets rise above the eastern horizon. These groups were divided into twelve in ancient times, to correspond with the months of the year, and they were given the names of animals and legendary creatures: Aries the ram, Taurus the bull, Gemini the twins, Cancer the crab, Leo the lion, Virgo the virgin, Libra the scales, Scorpio the scorpion, Sagittarius the archer, Capricorn the goat, Aquarius the water-bearer and Pisces the fish, in a cycle beginning in mid-March with the ancient New Year.

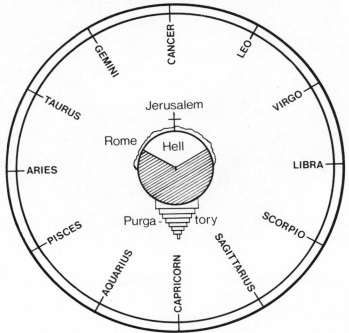

23. The Zodiac according to Dante.

It was of central importance to medieval thinking that all the influences which the universe exerted upon humanity should be seen to harmonize. The four 'humours' or characters, which were proper to the four elements—fire, earth, air and water—were matched with the signs of the Zodiac in turn. Aries, Leo and Sagittarius were thus all fire signs; Taurus, Virgo, Capricorn, earth signs; Gemini, Libra, Aquarius, air signs; and Cancer, Scorpio, Pisces, water signs. In addition Aries bore a warm moist 'complexion', Cancer a hot dry one, Libra a cold dry one and Capricorn a cold moist one because these signs marked the beginning of a new season.

To complicate matters further, the planets had to be made to fit into this system. While the apparent positions of the stars were affected by the earth's rotation round the sun, according to which they seemed to move more or less in a body, the movements of the planets conformed far less tidily with the scheme. Mars, for example, takes about two years to travel round the sun, and Jupiter about twelve. The problem was solved by allocating to each of the known planets (Uranus, Neptune and Pluto had not then been discovered) two Zodiac signs or 'houses' in which they exerted their strongest influence: for Mercury, Gemini and Virgo; for Venus, Libra and Taurus; for Mars, Aries and Scorpio; for Saturn, Sagittarius and Capricorn; and for Jupiter, Aquarius and Pisces. That left the Sun for Leo and the Moon for Cancer. When a planet coincided with one of its own signs of the zodiac, its power was at its height.

Because the visible heavens form more or less a hemisphere, not one but six signs are visible at once. It was the sign which was ascending, that is, just rising in the east, which dominated the Zodiac. The sign ascending at birth fixed a man's character for life. Even within a single day the influence of the planets was believed to change hour by hour, so that the third hour, for example, might belong to the moon.

Closely linked with this astrological scheme was the belief that the four 'elements' influenced human temperament. If everything was composed of earth, water, fire and air, including man himself, it seemed reasonable to look for explanations of a man's behaviour in his constitution. Earth, water, air, fire made a man respectively phlegmatic, melancholic, sanguine or choleric, according to which element predominated in his makeup. These four governing characteristics were known as the four 'humours' and each was associated with a body-fluid: phlegm, black bile, blood or yellow bile. The integration of the theory of the humours into this system meant that this hybrid science of astronomy and astrology was closely linked with the study of medicine. A good physician would take into account both sets of influences in deciding on his diagnosis. In a patient whose disease was caused by an excess of a certain humour, treatment might be expected to be most effective when that humour was not dominant in the stars, and thus even stronger in its hold over the patient. If a man's illness was believed to be caused by an imbalance of the humours, medical treatment must logically consist

24. These illustrations of medieval medical practice show a physician treating a swooning lady and surgeons performing an operation. (Bodleian MS. Ashmole 399 f. 33^r, 1462 f. 10^r)

of attempts to set that balance right. Too much blood caused a fever; the way to treat a fever victim was therefore to bleed him. A certain amount of advice was given by the text of the *Aphorisms* of the Greek physician, Hippocrates, and by other medical textbooks of Classical times; a good deal of medical practice was peculiarly medieval. A Moslem writer, Usamah, describes a scene which took place during the crusading period of the 12th century; a

Christian and a Moslem physician were presented with two patients:

> *a knight . . . in whose leg an abscess had grown, and a woman afflicted with imbecility. To the knight [the Moslem] applied a small poultice until the abscess opened and became well; and the woman [he] put on a diet and made her humour wet. Then a Frankish physician came to them and said, 'This man knows nothing about treating them.' He then said to the knight, 'Which wouldst thou prefer, living with one leg or dying with two?' The latter replied, 'Living with one leg.' The physician said, 'Bring me a strong knight and a sharp axe.' A knight came with the axe. And I was standing by. Then the physician laid the leg of the patient on a block of wood. [The leg was severed after some difficulty and the patient died on the spot.] He then examined the woman and said, 'This is a woman in whose head there is a devil which has possessed her. Shave off her hair.' [The woman did not recover, but became worse.] The physician then said, 'The Devil has penetrated through her head.' He therefore took a razor, made a deep cruciform incision on it, peeled off the skin in the middle of the incision until the bone of the skull was exposed, and rubbed it with salt. The woman also expired instantly.*[4]

The whole system was so complex in its ramifications and refinements that it was difficult for its exponents ever to be proved wrong; some additional influence could always be brought in to explain an apparent error. Faith in the system certainly seems to have been widespread, and not only belief, but a straightforward common habit of thinking in the terms of astrology. The Wife of Bath, by no means a learned woman, says that her character is compounded of the influences of Mars and Venus:

> *For certes, I am al Venerien*
> *In feelinge, and myn herte is Marcien.*
> *Venus me yaf my lust, my likerousnesse (licentiousness)*
> *And Mars yaf me my sturdy hardynesse.*

Mars, for example, was accredited with the qualities of the Roman god after which it was named, and those born under the influence of this planet were expected to develop into courageous and warlike adults, with, perhaps, a choleric temperament to match.

Chaucer's Doctor of Physic was grounded in '*astronomye*,' and is learned in his art, with its medical and astrological aspects:

He knew the cause of everich maladye,
Were it of hoot or coold, or moyste, or drye.

W. C. Curry describes the evidence for the view that Chaucer employs medical images, and a description of their respective humours in his portrayal of the Pardoner, the Reeve and Miller as well as of the Wife of Bath. Chaucer's own knowledge of the subject would presumably have been that of the ordinary educated man of his day, but he shows the same familiarity with the terminology and the experts that a modern man might possess if he read popular articles on medicine in newspapers and magazines. We may perhaps take it that the world at large was familiar with the principles of medieval medicine and with the notion of the humours and the power of the stars. No one appears to have felt that this 'science' was in any way fundamentally out of tune with Christian teaching.

The Canon's Yeoman, with his training in alchemy, belonged to a group of medieval scientists whose chief interest lay in discovering how to make gold from base metal. George Ripley of Bridlington is an example of a 15th century alchemist, but most of their names are lost, together with their abortive experiments. Alchemy may have been the distant ancestor of modern chemistry, but the resemblances are few. While a modern chemist conducts experiments to discover the chemical properties of certain substances, and to explore the effects of combining them in various ways, the medieval alchemist believed that he knew the end-product at which he was aiming. All his experiments were a means to an end, and the end and purpose was the discovery of a method of turning base metals into gold. Instead of trying to determine the essential nature of the elements—which would have taught him that his hopes were doomed—the alchemist mixed and heated and cooled, convinced that what he wanted was attainable; he had only to find the recipe. He believed that a key to the process lay in a fifth element (in addition to fire, water, earth and air) which was called the 'quintessence'. This would have the property of turning base metals into gold as if by magic, and was envisaged either as an elixir, or as a solid substance, the philosopher's stone, which is mentioned in the hymn:

This is the famous Stone
Which turneth all to gold.

The stone and the quintessence itself were also eagerly sought by the alchemists for this reason. There may be a parallel with modern interest in the properties and nature of the fourth dimension.

Medieval science may appear primitive by modern standards, but its principles and technicalities were every bit as complicated and obscure as those of its modern counterparts. Medieval science was in no sense the work of simple or stupid people; it engaged the best intellects of the day in lifetimes of concentrated study.

Fair comparison is impossible; medieval scientists began from a totally different set of assumptions which shaped their thinking quite differently from that of the modern scientist. Theory was all-important. Certain properties of the universe could not be otherwise than they were believed to be; ancient writers or the Bible itself appeared to have made statements which could not be gainsaid because of the immense authority they carried. Medieval scientists were primarily philosophers, and developed their theories simply by thinking them out, and not by testing them against experimental evidence. We tend to take it for granted now that scientific facts which are verified by experiments are true in an absolute sense, in much the same way as the medieval scientist attributed an absolute truth to his own views. But experiment can only test a hypothesis; it can never prove it beyond doubt, and scientific theory about the origin and behaviour of the universe, about medicine, about physics and chemistry is in a state of flux even now. We are not yet in a position to mock medieval scientists.

[1]From Latin text in M. Th. D'Alverney *Alain de Lille Textes Inédits* (Paris, 1967) p. 251   [2]C. G. Coulton *Life in the Middle Ages* (C.U.P., 1967) p. 43   [3]G. Leff *Mediaeval Thought* (Penguin, 1970) p. 119 [4]J. Kritzeck *Anthology of Islamic Literature* (Penguin, 1964) p. 217–8.

5

Chaucer the European

We can enjoy the literature of other countries only if we understand the language in which it is written. We can appreciate it fully only if we have a very thorough grasp of shades of meaning, idioms, ambiguities, colloquialisms. A mechanical knowledge of a foreign language is not enough. In Chaucer's day the boundaries between languages were far less clearly defined than they are now; the language of Chaucer's England was still comparatively close to that of France, and every educated man had some knowledge of Latin, which in its turn made Italian more accessible to him. The literary works which Chaucer particularly admired were written in languages which he must often have heard actually used, that is, in French, Latin and Italian. He borrowed plot, subject-matter, theme and even style from what he saw as models of excellence in writing.

Chaucer's travels may have brought a number of books into his hands, but even if he had spent his whole life in England he would have had the chance to read a good many of the popular romances written in France. He lived at a time when both serious scholarship and every kind of popular literature had an international flavour; an educated Englishman could meet an Italian or a Frenchman and find that they had enjoyed the same books and that they shared a common background of views about poetry.

25. An early 15th century picture of a party of riders out for amusement, from a French manuscript. The elaborate and colourful dress of both men and women, in particular their headgear, show them to be people of fashion and importance. Only those whose social class permitted were expected to wear fine clothes. It is for people such as these that the romances were still being copied and circulated. (BM MS. Harley 4431 f. 81)

Medieval poetical theory was derived from the technical skills of the classical poets. The common language of all scholars was still Latin. Schoolboys studied the Classical poets (Horace, Ovid, Virgil, in particular) with minute care. They learned to identify parts of speech and grammatical forms so as to improve their knowledge of the Latin language; but they also studied the poet's use of poetical devices such as metaphor, simile, personification, and in this way they learned to appreciate his technical skill. At the same time, they learned the names of the Classical gods and heroes, and the stories of their exploits. A whole cultural heritage went with the learning of Latin; Classical references flavour not only Chaucer's work, but that of Shakespeare, Milton, Pope, Keats, T.S. Eliot: the major poets of every century have drawn heavily on the Classical background which formed the basis of all education until comparatively recently.

Where we may be accustomed to studying the literatures of France, Germany, Spain or Italy separately, almost as an adjunct to the learning of the language in which they are written, Chaucer and his friends knew no such barriers to comparison.

Not merely the theory of the art of poetry, but also a good deal of practical technique was common to the poetry of every language. Poets borrowed each other's methods of composition. The same themes appear again and again, even whole passages are borrowed. It is important to remember that imitation, borrowing, and outright copying were not regarded as literary vices. In fact, the use of a previous author's best phrases, his most successful images, even his plot, was a perfectly acceptable, even an admirable practice. Medieval writers had an immense respect for the authorities, by whom they meant those authors who had gone before, in particular

26. This white-robed pilgrim is standing on a shore looking at a 'Ship of Religion'. Its white sails bear the sign of the cross and its red pennants denoted the blood of martyrdom. The manuscript from which the picture comes is a *Romance of the Pilgrimage of Man*. (Bodleian MS. Laud. Misc. 740 f. 118ᵛ)

the Classical and early Christian writers. A work heavily illustrated with quotations carried a certain authority of its own; in a similar way, a poem woven out of borrowed materials was felt to have a kind of richness lacking in an altogether new invention. Manuscript illumination of Chaucer's period is characterized by the ornately embroidered quality of its decoration; perhaps this reflects a similar pleasure in pattern, repetition and detail. In the early 19th century, Keats said that he felt that poetry should ideally be like a garden in which a man might stroll, repeatedly discovering new pleasures:

> *Do not the Lovers of Poetry like to have a little Region to wander in where they may pick and choose and in which the images are so numerous that many are forgotten and found new in a second reading: which may be food for a Week's Stroll in the Summer?*[1]

Poets of Chaucer's day took a similar pleasure in filling their verses with minutely detailed verbal embroidery. Scholars have never fully exhausted their search among the fund of references and borrowings hidden in his work. His poems are like tapestries rather than Impressionist paintings.

ROMANCE AND ALLEGORY

The French word for a novel, *roman*, comes from the same root as our 'romance'. The romances of Chaucer's day were stories, but there their similarity with the modern novel ends. The modern novel is normally written in prose; as a rule it tells a story which is unfamiliar to the reader, and it relies partly on the reader's desire to find out what happens to keep him reading to the end. There may be flashbacks or some juggling with the sequence of the plot, but the majority of novels keep more or less to the point, and, on a large scale, they tell a story. The romances were written in verse, and they often told a story whose essentials were already well-known to the audience. The audience's interest was not, therefore, to be captured by unexpected events. Instead, the medieval storyteller distracted his audience by means of digressions. He told every subordinate tale which came into his head. The result was a long poem which could be continued or left off or brought to an end, perhaps even as the response of the audience dictated. Sometimes these poems appear shapeless to the modern reader, mere strands of odds and ends loosely knitted up together. In fact their structure is often complicated, subtle and quite deliberate; but medieval ideas of literary form were very different from ours. The ancient Greeks had developed the notion of unity. The action of a play, they felt, should take place on a single day, with few characters, so that the dialogue could convey a crisis in one man's life with the greatest possible intensity. In contrast, the medieval writer's sprawling works explore every avenue, include every detail, entertain their audience by continually diverting it. Their purposes and their standards of excellence belong very much to their time.

Among the more commonly-used devices, which are far less familiar today, are allegories. An allegory tells a story, but it hides a deeper meaning under the plot and characters it describes. A symbolic character may represent an abstract idea, a place, a state of mind. John Bunyan used the same device in *The Pilgrim's Progress*, where Christian (who stands for every man's soul) meets Despair, Sloth, Vanity, Charity, Worldly-Wisdom and so on, in the guise of fellow-travellers, giants, even geographical features such as the Slough of Despond and the town of Vanity Fair. William Langland's poem *Piers Plowman* is an allegory in which the characters stand for virtues and vices and various human qualities.

Chaucer himself employs the device of allegory in *The Parliament of Fowls*. In a dream, the poet sees a beautiful park, or garden, where the birds have met to choose their mates; the goddess of Nature presides, and it is St Valentine's Day. The tercel eagle claims the formel eagle who sits on Nature's hand, but two other tercels, inferior in rank, dispute his claim. The three tercels argue their case before Nature, and then the dispute is debated by all the birds present, who have formed themselves into a parliament. Nature decides that the formel eagle shall make the choice for herself; she asks for a year in which to decide.

A number of theories have been advanced as explanations of this allegory. The most likely explanation is that Chaucer had in mind the events of 1381, when Richard II asked for the hand of Anne of Bohemia. The details do not fit exactly, however, so that it is possible that Chaucer was describing some other marriage suit within court circles. Critics are often led into long discussions over the exact interpretation of such allegories as this one and *The Book of the Duchess*, which presents fewer problems. But medieval writers did not necessarily go to a great deal of trouble to ensure that their allegories fitted reality at every point; an allegory more often carried a general moral, or was designed to match its parallel reality at only two or three points. It is, perhaps, dangerous to try to interpret too closely a literary device which was never designed to be treated in such a way.

The French romance had flowered in the 12th and 13th centuries. Epic poems, lays and lyrics, too, describe an idealized love which has come to be known as courtly love. The lover sighs for a lady who is unattainable, usually because she is married and the lover's honour forbids him to try to steal her from her lord. To win her favour, he performs feats of daring; he lays his trophies at her feet and she rewards him with a smile or a flower or perhaps a ribbon or glove, as a mark of her favour.

Medieval romances won their popularity in an age when marriages amongst the nobility were normally arranged; husband and wife had little or no choice in the matter. If the pair married young, they might come to love each other, but love was not felt to play an important part in marriage. A large number of young knights with no control of their family lands as yet, or perhaps younger sons, must have been hangers-on at many courts. Without property it was unlikely that they would marry; a devotion to the unattainable lady of a man of higher rank provided a relatively safe emotional outlet.

The Church's attitude to women was ambivalent. On the one hand, women were regarded as daughters of Eve, temptresses, vessels of wickedness; their proper place was in humble submission to their husbands. On the other hand, the Church held up the example of the Blessed Virgin Mary as an ideal among women, deserving of a respect which amounted almost to worship. The lady of the chivalric knight clearly resembles the Virgin Mary in that she is not treated as a real woman, but as an idealized figure.

Since it is the romances themselves which provide the bulk of the surviving evidence as to the nature and rules of courtly love, it is extremely difficult to determine the realities of life at those courts where the romances were popular. It is probable that the brightness of the ideal was often tarnished; it is probable that the harsh realities of war bred men of rougher habits and less polished manners than these stories would suggest. Nevertheless, the popularity of the romances suggests that they fulfilled a demand; the ideal at least was one which appealed to the courtly audience.

In *The Allegory of Love*, C. S. Lewis suggests that there were four essential conditions for courtly love: humility in the would-be lover; courtesy of behaviour and bearing, with all that the term then implied; adultery (the lady was always married to someone else) and a 'religion of love' which elevated the feelings of the lover to a spiritual plane.

In many short lyric poems, the lover is a knight or a wandering scholar who comes upon an innocent girl in the fields and seduces her. The arguments he uses form the subject-matter of the poem. There is often a polished wit, an elegant dryness in these lyrics. The whole composition is neatly turned, and put together with a professional skill. The writers of such songs and verses were often professionals who provided the members of a patron's court with amusing popular songs, as well as entertaining them with the narratives of mighty deeds done by noblemen like themselves in an artificially dangerous world of demons and dragons.

Guillaume de Machaut was among the French poets who appear to have had a strong influence on Chaucer. A stanza of one of his ballads provides a typical example of the conventions of this kind of poetry:

> Se je vous aim de fin loyal courage
> Et ai amé et amerai toudis,
> Et vous avez pris autre en mariage,
> Dois je pour ce de vous estre en sus mis
> Et de tous poins en oubli?
> Certes, nennil; car puis que j'ai en mi
> Cuer si loyal qu'il ne savroit meffaire,
> Vous ne devez vo cuer de moi retraire.[2]

> [If I love you with a true heart, and have loved you, and always shall do so, and you have taken another man in marriage, must I for that be sent away from you and quite forgotten? No, no, indeed, for since I have in me a heart so loyal that it could do no ill, you must not take your heart away from me.]

For the modern taste, this may seem to be lacking in spontaneity; but such poetry was written with an eye for elegance and the formality which was much admired by lovers of the art. Medieval taste appreciated demonstrations of sheer technical skill, whose excellence the initiated could fully perceive.

The Roman de la Rose was probably the most influential of all the works of the French poets. It is an ornate story beginning with a long passage of description which sets the scene in a rose garden. A lover meets his lady at the pool of Narcissus. A complex allegory follows in which the rose garden, the pool, and the god of love with his weapons are given a variety of symbolical meanings. Among those found in the garden is Oiseuse or leisure, Deduit, who owns the garden and who personifies delight, Raison or reason and Jalosie or jealousy. Such personified vices, virtues and human qualities argue with the lover in a meandering debate. There is no

27. These illustrations are from a manuscript of the *Roman de la Rose*. The first shows the pagan god of love, winged and crowned. Chaucer, in *The Franklin's Tale* describes how love cannot be forced. When one of the lovers tries to dominate the other, love vanishes:

> *Love wol nat been constreyned by maistrye.*
> *When maistrye comth, the God of Love annon*
> *Beteth his wynges, and farewel, he is gon!*

This winged god of love is a very different figure from the baby Cupid of Renaissance art. The bottom picture shows two people in a garden. Medieval formal gardens provided raised turf seats, like the one in this picture, on which walkers could sit to talk. (Bodleian MS. Seld. Supra 57 f. 6ᵛ, f. 150ᵛ) attempt to follow a neat plan without digression. When the story-teller comes to a mention of, for example, Narcissus, he tells the legend of Narcissus at length.

Chaucer's early poem, *The Book of the Duchess*, owes a great deal to this poem. He, too, describes a dream in which the hero wakes up to walk through the countryside until he comes upon an earthly paradise (the garden); both authors mention Macrobius' *Comment-ary on the Dream of Scipio* as a prelude to their own descriptions of dreams. The parallels are numerous. Certain themes—the magic-al garden, the talking birds, and the dream, for example—are common to French courtly poetry and to a number of Chaucer's works.

His *The Parliament of Fowls*, as we have seen, consists of a debate among a group of birds in a magical garden on the subject of love. Examples of such visions of love, or dreams, appear in *Troilus and Criseyde* and in *The Nun's Priest's Tale*. There are 'gardens of love' or magic gardens in the *Prologue* to *Legend of*

28. A lady and servant in a garden. They appear to be sitting in a bower, and the garden is sown with flowers among the grass, as seems to have been common in medieval gardens. '*All full of fresshe flowers as is a mead.*' The conventional gardens of love poetry were idealized versions of such real gardens as the illuminators of manuscripts draw for us. (Bodleian MS. Rawl. Liturg. e 36 f. 2ᵛ)

Good Women, and in *The Franklin's Tale* and *The Merchant's Tale*. The Black Knight who appears in the *Roman de la Rose* was probably the model for some of the lovers whom Chaucer invents, especially, perhaps for Troilus. The 'lover's complaint' or the lover's description of his own sufferings occurs in *Troilus*, in *The Knight's Tale*, in *The Squire's Tale*. This is a device common in French poetry. Chaucer also enjoys indulging in elaborate descriptions, another feature of such poetry.

The influence of French poetry on Chaucer is evident then, throughout his writing. It furnished him with a number of convenient themes, and coloured his poetic imagination. He writes as a poet of his time, to whom the most obvious literary models were to be found in the *Roman de la Rose* and other works of French poets such as Guillaume de Machaut and Froissart. (Jean Froissart spent some years in the royal household in the 1360s as the Queen's secretary. He and Chaucer must have known each other.)

The influence of the Italian poets is of a rather different kind, but there is no doubt that it is present. Giovanni Sercambi's *Novelle* may have been known to Chaucer. It too consists of a collection of stories told by a group of people going on pilgrimage, and possibly provided Chaucer with the unifying theme he needed for his own collection of stories. Petrarch, Boccaccio and Dante, the great poets of medieval Italy must have exerted a profound influence on anyone who read them: Boccaccio, and Petrarch, provided Chaucer with plots for the stories he puts into the mouths of his pilgrims. *The Knight's Tale*, for example, is adapted from Boccaccio's *Teseide; The Clerk's Tale* is Petrarch's story, *De Obedientia ac Fide Uxoria Mythologa (On the Mythical Obedience and Faithfulness of Wives)*. Petrarch took the story (which he wrote in Latin) from Boccaccio. *The Franklin's Tale* is substantially the same as one of Boccaccio's stories. *The Monk's Tale* takes its plan from Boccaccio. In the second Nun's 'Invocation of Mary' there are elements drawn from Dante's *Paradiso*.

Chaucer was a younger contemporary of Petrarch and Boccaccio; when he read their works he was reading freshly-written material which had been only comparatively recently published. Publication for a medieval author meant a process of copying and distribution which was bound to be to some extent haphazard. Books must have been recommended by friends, heard of through acquaintances; new works might become popular at court, but only because some member of the court circle had discovered them for himself and introduced them to his friends. It was perfectly possible for a man like Chaucer, who clearly read a good deal of contemporary literature, and perhaps liked to keep up with the latest books, to know only some of the writings of a contemporary author. The manuscript volumes he owned or borrowed from friends might contain only a part of a favourite author's works, and it could be a lengthy and difficult task to obtain other works by the same author. There were no professional reviewers of books, no catalogues of books in print, none of the modern machinery which enables a reader to order almost any book he may want, wherever in the world it happens to have been published.

This limitation on the circulation of books in Chaucer's day may help to explain one of the apparently curious aspects of his knowledge of the work of the Italian poets. *The Knight's Tale* is based on Boccaccio's *Teseide*, and *Troilus* draws on *Filostrato* and *Filocolo;* yet it is perfectly possible that Chaucer had not read the *Decameron*. Presumably, therefore, he had access to a volume which contained only some of Boccaccio's poems. The *Decameron* would have had a lively appeal for Chaucer. It has something in common with *The Canterbury Tales* in its overall plan and structure. Seven young ladies and three young men retire to their country estates to avoid the plague which seized Florence and much of the rest of Europe in 1348. For ten days the young people tell each other stories, at the rate of ten stories a day. The last story, the one which is given pride of place, is the tale of Patient Griselda, which Chaucer put into the mouth of the Clerk. Yet Chaucer's knowledge of this story does not apparently come from Boccaccio, but from Petrarch.

Boccaccio met Petrarch in 1350; Petrarch had a love of the Latin Classics which coloured his writing and led him to write the Latin prose version of the Griselda story which Chaucer knew and used. Although unlikely, it is not impossible that Chaucer himself may have met Petrarch; in 1373 Chaucer was on his mission to Genoa, and Padua would not have been far out of his way. It must have been in such ways that the poets of the day exchanged themes and subjects for their writing: through meetings and talk, as well as in written form, the gradual diffusion of poetical material went on. Many of the stories he uses could have come to Chaucer's ears indirectly because they were commonly known: Boccaccio's version of a tale may have been told him by a friend. It is impossible to be sure exactly what Chaucer had read for himself. What is perhaps of the greatest interest is his willingness to fashion his tales out of these and a dozen other sources, to weave an assortment of material drawn from what to us seem different cultures into a literary whole with a character of its own.

Chaucer borrows, too, from his knowledge of Classical works, as well as from the Latin writers of the Middle Ages, from Alan of Lille's *The Complaint of Nature*, for example. (Alan of Lille was a scholar-poet of the late 12th century, whose epic allegories depended heavily on his Classical learning for their ideas and imagery.) Everything Chaucer read was grist to his mill, as it was to Shakespeare. Each made something distinctively his own out of what he used. Chaucer's audience would certainly have been more impressed by an old tale well-told than by a new one half-formed; they would appreciate the technical skills and the added graces of the author's refashioning.

[1]M. B. Forman (Ed.) *The Letters of John Keats* no. 25 (O.U.P., 1952) p. 52   [2]B. Woledge (Ed.) *Penguin Book of French Verse* vol. I, *To the Fifteenth Century* (Penguin, 1968) p. 224.

6

The Canterbury Tales: Tales and Tellers

Chaucer's characters are drawn from every rank of society, from clergy and from laity, from town and country. But the distribution is uneven; even allowing for the wide range of occupations and vocations which were embraced by the clerical profession, the clergy occupy a disproportionate place. There are few characters who come from the poorer classes, who would probably have been less articulate, less skilled in the art of storytelling, and would therefore have made less varied and lively contributions to the tale-telling. There is no reason to suppose that Chaucer intended to provide an actual sample of the population of 14th century England.

The range of variation in Chaucer's treatment of his characters is perhaps more significant than the range of ranks and professions in the characters themselves. Those whose fellows Chaucer would probably have known best in his own daily life are portrayed with a shrewdness and subtlety which reveals both their failings and their individual merits, and makes them credible human beings. Chaucer's portraits of the Merchant, the Franklin, the Shipman, are portraits of members of his own social class, of men with whom he might himself have had dealings. When he describes members of the nobility—the Knight, the Squire—or certain of the churchmen, he is more inclined to give us a stylized rendering of a type, rather than a real person. A medieval writer would have found nothing discordant in such a mingling of roundly characterized individuals with cardboard figures.

The majority of Chaucer's characters have no names; Daun Piers the monk and Harry Bailly the Host, for example, travel with a band of people distinguished only by their positions in society, or by the careers they pursue. In the Middle Ages a man's identity was much more a matter of position and status than of individual personality. Names are of secondary importance to Chaucer; his pilgrims are individuals even where they are not named.

THE GOOD

THE KNIGHT

Among Chaucer's company, the highest in rank or degree of the laymen is the Knight. He has fought on crusade, that is, in a holy war. The number of occasions on which he has taken part in battles suggests that he is not in the service of a single lord, but a mercenary who offered his services in any worthy cause. It has been shown that he could in fact have fought on all the campaigns which Chaucer mentions, but there is perhaps no need to look for so close a correspondence with reality. What is important here is his eagerness to come on pilgrimage as soon as he returns from his latest expedition—while the rust-stains from his armour are still visible on his clothes. He is a genuinely pious man. Chaucer has only good to say of him. He is an example of the *'parfit gentil knyght'*, a gentleman in the medieval sense of the word. He possesses the finest knightly qualities. He loves *'trouthe and honour, fredom and curteisie'*. Although he is not lacking in courage, and always kills his man, he is by no means a violent man, but gentle and courteous:

> *And of his port as meeke as is a mayde.*
> *He nevere yet no vileynye ne sayde*
> *In al his lyf unto no maner wight.*

This delicate balance of fine feeling, self-restraint, honour, courage and energy make up the medieval notion of the quality of *'gentilesse'*, which is proper to the nobleman; it is an important theme of *The Franklin's Tale*. The knight exemplifies the finest qualities of ideal knighthood. Chaucer himself had been present on the battlefield and as a young man had experienced the brutalities of medieval warfare at first hand. He cannot have intended the portrait of the Knight to represent knighthood as he must have seen it in action. The Knight is intended to set an example in keeping with a literary rather than a real picture of knighthood.

THE SQUIRE

The Squire who accompanies the Knight—his own son— is a young man who promises to become an equally fine knight. He has already proved himself in Flanders, Artois and Picardy, where he has acquitted himself well, although he is not yet twenty-one, the traditional age at which he would have been made a knight. Like a true knight in the tradition of courtly love, he has fought bravely in order to please his lady: *'In hope to stonden in his lady grace'*. Not only does he ride well, but he also displays a mastery of the courtly arts of singing and dancing. While his father has all the merits and solid virtues of mature knighthood, the Squire displays all the graces of young knighthood. Above all, he possesses that joyousness which was considered a virtue in the young knight. All day long he sings: *'He was as fressh as is the month of May.'* We are explicitly told that he is *'curteis'*; his *'curteisye'* embraces both the modern sense of the term 'courtesy', and its medieval sense of true knightliness. Again, he is a type; he exemplifies all the proper qualities of the promising young knight.

THE YEOMAN

The Yeoman who accompanies father and son is barely sketched as a character. His appearance is described in some detail: With his sheaf of arrows fledged with peacock-feathers and his green clothing, he evokes a figure in a book illumination. We learn only that he is a good forester, a strong man used to an open-air life, and thoroughly serviceable to the Knight. He owes his place in the *General Prologue* to the fact that it would seem only proper for such a knight travelling with his squire to have a servant of a slightly lower degree to accompany him. In this way, the Knight's company as a whole provides an edifying opening spectacle for the audience of the *General Prologue*. The little party sets a tone of moral uprightness without sententiousness; the descriptions of the Squire and the Yeoman reinforce the general impression Chaucer seeks to make on his readers in the characterization of the Knight. The party is treated as a unified whole, in which there is nothing out of tune.

Only two members of the party tell their stories. The Knight's tale is entirely in keeping with his modesty and uprightness of character; he makes it clear that he admires his hero Theseus for his knightliness, and is disgusted by Creon's *'vileinye'*. The people he describes are aristocratic, and the story he tells is one of romance and adventure. Theseus is a character from an 'old story' (although to Chaucer and his contemporaries he is also a historical character). If the Knight had time, he would tell us in detail about his successful battles, the story of his winning of Hippolyta the Amazon Queen, *'And of the feste that was at hire weddynge'*. All this is traditional subject matter of the epic poem. Theseus' banner bears the device of Mars, the Roman god of war. Thus the Knight sets his tale in Classical times, but gives it all the familiar trappings of the knighthood of his own day. The tale of Palamon and Arcite which follows is Chaucer's adaptation of the *Teseide* of Boccaccio. The Italian poet had already made the Greek story medieval. Chaucer shortens it, reshapes it, and puts it into the mouth of his Knight, who is the best-fitted of his characters to tell it.

The *Squire's Tale* is a typical romance, for which Chaucer's source, if he had one, has never been found. The story is unfinished —perhaps Chaucer was unable to complete the plan to his own satisfaction; perhaps the break is allowed to stand as an amusing interruption in its own right. It has been suggested that he owes the oriental setting to his reading of *The Travels of Marco Polo*, but whatever influences may have helped to give the tale its present form, it is beautifully tailored to fit the character of the Squire, both in its subject-matter and in its grace of style and treatment. It would be fitting that the Squire should be a fluent and elegant storyteller, as well as a fine singer; the skill would be another asset to the young courtier.

Chaucer abandons the tale with the Franklin's words of praise to the Squire:

> In feith, Squier, thow hast thee well yquit
> And gentilly. I preise wel thy wit.

The Franklin is impressed; he wishes that his own son were a young man with the Squire's qualities, so that he might learn '*gentillesse*' (a coveted attribute, evidently, in the Franklin's circle). The Franklin's respect for gentlemanly qualities and for good breeding may perhaps have been sharpened by his own awareness of a slight inferiority in his own social position. Nevertheless, there is no sign of any lack of the social skills in the consummate ease with which he interrupts the Squire's prolixities after only two lines of the third part of his tale.

THE CLERK

Chaucer gives us two exemplary figures from among the clergy, perhaps to balance his, on the whole, unflattering portraits of other members of the clergy. Chaucer was too sane a man for there to be acrimony or lack of tolerance in his attitude to any single group of his characters. The Clerk is a student at the University of Oxford (and, like his fellow-students, he is to be counted a member of the clergy). He is a wandering scholar who has been at Padua. Medieval students travelled all over Europe in search of the best masters. The Clerk is a serious student, thin and pale, a man who prefers the pursuit of learning to the pursuit of wealth.

He would rather have twenty books—a sizeable private library in Chaucer's day—than the fine clothes he might earn in one of the professions. Unlike the majority of his fellows, he has not left the university after taking his bachelor's degree. It was quite usual for an ambitious young man to set out at that point to make his career in the Church or the civil service.

Chaucer's Clerk has long since begun the study of logic, which suggests that he may have been studying for his Master's degree. Medieval university courses normally lasted, like apprenticeships, for seven years, and students of theology in particular, and those who wanted to become Doctors of Theology, Law or Medicine might still be students well into middle age. So Chaucer's Clerk is not necessarily a very young man. He speaks little, and when he speaks he talks quickly and nervously, yet with a scholar's love of fine words and precision of expression:

> *Noght o word spak he moore than was neede,*
> *And that was seyde in forme and reverence,*
> *And short and quyk and ful of hy sentence.*

His tale has a scholarly theme, that of the nature of true obedience and faithfulness in a good wife. Chaucer took the tale from Petrarch's rendering of Boccaccio's story, or perhaps from Boccaccio himself, but his wording is often very close to Petrarch's Latin version, so this seems the more likely source. Patient Griselda suffers persecutions; she has her children taken away from her and is sent away in disgrace. But she comes through her temptations triumphantly. It is a moral tale, well-suited to the character of so earnest, serious and ascetic a clerk. The Clerk makes no bones about his borrowing of the story; like all medieval scholars he feels that his tale gains authority from its source. To acknowledge that it is the work of '*Frounceys Petrak*' only adds to its impressiveness; he feels no shame in acknowledging that the tale is not his own.

THE PARSON

The Parson is the second of Chaucer's idealized clerical figures. He is humble, virtuous, conscientious in his work—a holy man. He has learning enough to teach his parishioners the doctrines of the faith and to preach sermons, a degree of scholarship which was by no means universal among members of the ordinary parish clergy. They were sometimes grossly ignorant men, barely literate and wholly uninstructed in liturgy or doctrine. He bears trouble patiently and gives so generously of his meagre income to those of his parishioners who are in need that he leaves himself scarcely enough to live on. The incomes from such 'benefices' as the Parson's parish varied enormously. Those who had a rich parish to offer found plenty of candidates for the living ready to hand. Poorer parishes were likely to find it difficult to attract such a priest as Chaucer's Parson and many incumbents were far from conscientious in carrying out their duties.

Chaucer's Parson has none of those vices of the parish clergy with which Chaucer was clearly familiar. He sets a good example to his flock and does his own duties, instead of handing them over to someone else for a fee while himself going off to London in search of a richer benefice. With his parishioners he is mild and gentle, encouraging them to follow his example, but when he meets with a stubborn sinner he knows how to be severe. He embodies the priestly virtues to such a degree that Chaucer can only have meant him to be regarded as an ideal type; perhaps to make a sharp contrast with the more obvious abuses current among the parish clergy. The Parson's character is built up by means of a series of contrasts with the behaviour of those real priests who were responsible for such abuses.

The Host suspects the Parson of being a Lollard; but the Parson does not exemplify the more extreme views of the Lollards, only those qualities which the most uncontroversial reform would have produced: simple Christian virtues. The Parson does not make attacks on the behaviour of the higher clergy, or on the system of indulgences, or on the use the Church makes of the gifts of pilgrims to the shrines of saints. But he embodies those priestly excellencies which the Lollards found lacking in so many of the clergy.

His tale is long—a sermon on penitence, told in prose, and very far from being the '*merry tale*' he promises when he begins. Perhaps he is merely making a modest jest. The tale contains (as a separate unit within its overall construction), something very like a treatise on the Seven Deadly Sins. The work appears in many ways uncharacteristic of Chaucer, and its authenticity has been suspected. But a single immediate source has not been found, although treatises of this general type were well-known. The Latin chapter-headings and divisions in particular resemble those commonly found in manuscripts of similar works. In manuals for preachers and in sermons themselves the vices and virtues were treated as suitable topics for preaching. The preacher was able to draw on a stock collection of relevant quotations from early Christian writers such as St Jerome, St Augustine, St Gregory, in order to give authority to his remarks. The subject of a given vice or virtue might serve as subject-matter for a whole sermon, or it might be brought in as a moral in a sermon composed for a special feast-day, such as the Nativity or Palm Sunday. Such collections of useful material were therefore very necessary to the preacher in an age when books were not indexed for easy reference, and when in any case a full reference library was beyond the means of an ordinary parson. The Parson, then, gives a detailed exposition of his subject.

It has been argued that the whole body of *The Canterbury Tales* was designed to explicate the Parson's theme of the Seven Deadly Sins, and that his tale, coming at the end, was intended to provide a serious commentary on what had gone before. It certainly contrasts strongly, in length and in seriousness, with many of Chaucer's tales.

THE BAD

The ideally good of its kind is a concept perhaps as easily recognizable to us as it was to medieval people. We can accept that a man may be a very good knight because he possesses all the knightly virtues, or a very good parson because he possesses all the virtues appropriate to the clergyman. The principle cannot, however, be applied so easily in reverse. The absolutely evil is a very different proposition. Shakespeare's villains all have some redeeming weakness, with the exception perhaps of Iago, in *Othello*, whose ruthlessness seems to have no softening quality. Chaucer describes a Friar whose failings as a friar make him both a bad man and a bad friar, and yet he does not intend to hold him up as an example of unrelieved wickedness. The Summoner and the Pardoner are perhaps closer to being personifications of absolute evil.

THE SUMMONER

The Summoner's profession was to bring offenders to justice before the Church courts. The scope for corrupt practices which such an office provided is only too obvious. He would have found it easy to grow rich on the bribes he was offered, and to take every advantage of the fear of his intended victims. The Friar describes a Summoner of vicious habits at the beginning of his tale. Chaucer makes his own Summoner a stylized figure whose appearance signifies his wickedness. His fiery-red face suggests his affinity with hell—as well as his lecherous nature. He has a hideously disfiguring skin disease, which cannot be eased by any known remedy. The inward condition of his soul may be said to be represented by the outward condition of his skin. He is not entirely sane. He wears a loaf or a cake as a shield, and a garland on his head; his appearance terrifies every child he meets. The link between insanity and wickedness is familiar in medieval thinking. The mentally sick were thought to be possessed by devils; the good were those whose lives were in harmony with the universe, whose minds were at peace, those who were sound and whole and sane. *The Summoner's Tale* amounts to an attack on his enemy the Friar; he describes the Friars' deceitful methods of begging. The friars did not enjoy a good reputation, and no doubt the Summoner had brought many friars to court; there is certainly no love lost between the two; the Friar meets the Summoner's attack with one of his own.

THE PARDONER

The Pardoner who accompanies the Summoner is his counterpart in evil. If the Summoner stands for hell, the Pardoner stands for death. He is, as G. L. Kittredge has said, a lost soul, but rather more than that, he is a living symbol of his own damnation. He is dressed in a cap with a badge of St Veronica upon it—a face of Christ, like that which was believed to have been imprinted upon St Veronica's handkerchief when she wiped His face on the way to Calvary. The Pardoner carries false relics. In contrast with these apparent symbols of his clerical profession, he wears his hair long and yellow, loose about his shoulders, and his head uncovered. His hood, which as a member of the clergy he should wear on his head for propriety's sake, is bundled up in his wallet. He is a beardless and effeminate creature, neither man nor woman, and thus an offence to medieval minds. Everything about him rings false; in every respect he turns out to be other than he seems.

He is perfectly conscious of his own villainy, as he freely admits in the prologue to his tale. Although he is a wicked man, he proposes to tell a moral tale—again, his actions belie his words. His frank confession is made entirely without shame; it is in no way designed to win our sympathy, but rather to show his lack of any redeeming feature, even of the capacity to feel shame for his misbehaviour.

The Pardoner has no exact modern counterpart. His official task was to sell 'indulgences'. It was believed that the Church possessed a store of the virtue of the saints, which the faithful could buy to increase the weight of their own goodness, or to help wipe out their sins. Not everyone who claimed to be a pardoner had an official licence, and Chaucer's Pardoner in particular is a caricature of all the worst members of this profession. He carries a wallet full of pardons '*comen from Rome al hoot*', and several false relics to add verisimilitude to his claims—a pillowcase which purports to be the veil of the Virgin Mary and a glass vessel which contains only the bones of a pig. He can read a lesson in church, or sing, to such purpose that he wins over his listeners and makes fools of them all, selling his pardons easily to the gullible: '*He made the person and the peple his apes.*' He sings the offertory best, because he knows it is the 'song' which will win him generous offerings.

Chaucer describes the Pardoner and his companion the Summoner last in the list of pilgrims. Maurice Hussey has aptly called them 'damned souls' and certainly Chaucer's irony turns to the bitterest of sarcasm when he describes these men; there is no gentle, affectionate prodding at their human failings, but a biting condemnation.

The Pardoner's Tale is an *exemplum*, an illustration of a kind much used by preachers. He has worked it up into a tale but its purpose would originally have been to encourage those who heard a sermon to abandon the vices of gluttony and self-indulgence. There is a heavy irony here, since the Pardoner is himself clearly addicted at least to the second of these vices. But the tale is perfectly in character; the Pardoner would have developed a considerable facility in telling such stories in the course of his experience in preaching. Appropriately enough, the plot of the tale concerns three drunken revellers who plan to kill Death himself, and are tricked into killing each other.

THE FRIAR

The Friar is another of Chaucer's wicked men, but his wickedness is of a quite different kind from that of the Summoner and the Pardoner. He is a lover of pleasure, indulgent to his penitents at a price, sociable—he is '*famulier*', at his ease, with the wealthy and influential men of his neighbourhood. He, too, is lecherous, and carries little gifts for ladies in his *typet* or cape. He is corrupt, but not perhaps intended as a symbol of absolute evil.

The friars, or mendicants, were wandering members of one of the four orders of friars which existed in 14th century England: the Dominicans, Franciscans, Carmelites and Augustinians. Unlike the monks and nuns, their vows did not bind them to remain within monastery walls. Their founders' original intentions had been that they should live like Christ himself—poor, and dependent for food and shelter on the kindness and hospitality of strangers. In return, they should preach and do what good works they could. The mendicant life soon attracted men who saw in it an easy and a pleasurable existence, with some prestige and few responsibilities. Chaucer's Friar does not occupy an important position in his order. He evidently belongs to that large body of friars who were viewed by the population as troublemakers—and with some justification. Friars were often to be found at the bottom of disturbances: if, for example, a group of journeymen broke away from their gild and tried to set up a rival 'trade union', a friar might encourage them with promises to get the Church's official blessing for the enterprise —for a fee.

The Friar lives on his wits and his tongue, and we might therefore expect him to be a fluent talker. His tale is directed against the Summoner; it is the story of a trick played by the Devil, in this case upon a rascally Summoner, although similar tales have a judge or a lawyer as hero—any man who has authority to abuse, and whose greed or pomposity makes him a deserving target for punishment.

FRIENDS AND NEIGHBOURS

When Chaucer describes members of his own class, a new subtlety enters into his writing. No longer does he simply illustrate the virtues of the ideal knight or point out the flaws in the character of a bad man: the Merchant, the Sergeant of Law and the Franklin have lively personalities with the small failings and modest skills of recognizable people. Some may even have been modelled on people Chaucer knew. The method of characterization here is altogether more sophisticated and perhaps more masterly.

THE MERCHANT

The Merchant is the first of these representatives of the middle classes. His clothing is fashionable and expensive, his bearing impressive:

> *In mottelee and hye on horse he sat;*
> *Upon his head a Flaundryssh bever hat,*
> *His boots clasped faire and fetisly.*

In dignified tones, he describes his business affairs and boasts that he never loses money in a venture. In a medieval sense he plays the stock market. But his talk merely provides a front; the Merchant is in debt. His excursions into the world of international

29. These merchants appear to be watching their ships come in. (Bodleian MS. Bodl. 401 f. 55ᵛ)

finance and his activities as an extortionate money-lender have not always paid off. Chaucer would have known many such dealers, financiers and traders (or merchant-venturers). The Merchant seems to combine all three professions. It has been suggested that his portrait describes a certain Gilbert Maghfield, or one of the merchants of the Staple, who traded chiefly in wool. The description might have been immediately recognizable to Chaucer's audience; or perhaps it is a composite portrait. But into a small compass, Chaucer compresses many of the features of the life and work of the merchant class.

The Merchant's Tale, then, is told by a worried business man who desires to put a good face on his affairs, and to show himself in the best possible light. He chooses a story about marriage because, as he tells the company, he knows only too well what it is to have a shrewish wife: '*I now heere/Koude tellen of my wyves cursednesse!*' (He has been married only two months.) His hero, a man of sixty, takes a wife in his old age. In the Merchant's eyes, such a wife is: '*the fruyt of his tresor*', the most valuable among the possessions he has amassed, a sign of his wealth and position; in this way Chaucer shapes the tale to suit the Merchant's character and the opinions appropriate to him.

The Merchant shakes his head over the morals of the younger generation:

> *They lyve but as a bryd or as a beest,*
> *In libertee, and under noon arreest.*

They have no self-discipline, because they have no responsibilities, he claims. The view is not unfamiliar today.

His tale of January, his young wife May, and her lover, Damian, and the trick the lovers play upon May's old husband, is largely Chaucer's own invention, although, as we might expect, he introduces elements which are to be found in other contemporary stories. But the tale as the Merchant tells it expresses the attitude, which we may suppose to be characteristic of his class, that the possession of a fine wife is a sign of a man's status in the world. His own views on love and marriage may seem grounded in an almost cynical realism when compared with the more fanciful picture conveyed by *The Knight's Tale* and that of the Squire. The Merchant's characters display the fine scruples proper to characters in the courtly love stories: the lover, Damian, is a humble suitor; his lady, May, receives him with pity and graciousness; he wins her love by means of his services and gentleness of manner. But the Merchant's cynicism breaks through the conventions of the contemporary love-story. Not only May's marriage to January, but also the feeling between the lovers is shown to contain elements of ruthlessness, selfishness and harshness.

THE SERGEANT OF LAW

Chaucer's Sergeant of Law is another middle class figure. Today he would be a barrister of many years' experience; sergeants-at-law were chosen from among the barristers who had practised for sixteen years. In Chaucer's time only about twenty such officials existed; the Sergeant of Law is therefore a man of considerable importance. Attempts have been made to identify him with Thomas Pynchbek, the most likely candidate among the sergeants of Chaucer's day. Chaucer's sergeant often presides as a judge in court: '*Justice he was ful often in assise*'. Chaucer hints that the Sergeant has taken fat fees for arranging transactions in land-purchase. He has a fluent command of his subject: '*And every statut koude he pleyn by rote*'. (He knows the laws by heart.) There is a bustling self-importance about his manner which makes him appear to be busier than he is:

> *Now her so bisy a man as he ther nas,*
> *And yet he semed bisier than he was.*

(Here Chaucer slips in a comment which only the poet could make, and not the character 'Chaucer' who is present on the pilgrimage and who acts as observer.)

The Man of Law's prologue is little more than a rendering of Pope Innocent III's tract, *On Despising the World*, and it seems to have little connection with the tale which follows. It is possible that the 'translation' itself was originally meant to be *The Man of Law's Tale*, and that *The Tale of Constance* was introduced later. Here Chaucer was probably still shaping his composition. *The Tale of Constance* itself is borrowed from Nicholas Trivet's *Anglo-Norman Chronicle* of 1335. Chaucer's friend, John Gower, used the same story in his *Lover's Confession* (*Confessio Amantis*). Chaucer had already told the stories of a number of other such women in his *Legend of Good Women*, which is a collection of tales of women of the past who were famous for their virtue, or for their endurance in the face of temptation or tribulation. The story of Constance does not appear in the *Legend* itself. Perhaps Chaucer came across the story later, and thought it suitable for the Man of Law. He may have adapted it from an early draft, adding appropriate moralizing and philosophical reflections to suit it to the lips of a man who is accustomed to having his lightest word taken seriously, and whose position gives him scope to pontificate upon the failings of the world.

THE FRANKLIN

The Franklin has a great house, and at heart he is a country gentleman. He is not quite a nobleman, but it seems that he would have occupied a position of respect in his neighbourhood. As his story shows, he has an immense respect for the noble quality of '*gentillesse*', and it is possible that he feels acutely his lack of aristocratic birth and background in the company of some of the other pilgrims. But he is a man of importance in his own right, sheriff of his county, an office that made him the chief administrative official of the king in the county. The Franklin has been a Member of Parliament, and he is the Sergeant of Law's travelling companion, which in itself is a proof of his standing. His genial hospitality shows him to be a man who enjoys good food, fine wine and good company. Chaucer calls him an Epicurean—even in his time the term had lost its original meaning of a follower of the philosophical system of the Greek philosopher Epicurus. Only one aspect of Epicurus' teaching had survived, in a distorted form, and that was the belief that he taught his followers to seek pleasure. The Franklin is certainly an 'Epicurean' in the sense of 'a lover of pleasure'. He '*heeld opinioun that pleyn delit/Was verraily felicitee parfit.*'

His tale resembles the lays or narrative poems of the French poetess Marie de France, who wrote at the end of the 12th century.

She claimed that her stories came from Brittany: *The Franklin's Tale* is set in Brittany, and he himself calls it a lay. But the story is not borrowed from Marie de France, and no single source for it has ever been found. The characters who appear in *The Franklin's Tale* are of the highest birth, and for the most part their conduct is '*gentil*' to a fault. The Franklin's story thus perhaps matches his social aspirations, but the point should not be pressed too far. The tale is certainly one of Chaucer's more finely-polished stories, as we should expect of a teller who is able to bring the Squire's complicated tale so tactfully to a halt.

THE SHIPMAN

As the son of a wine merchant, Chaucer would have known a number of shipmen, or ship's captains, in his boyhood. His father would have had dealings with both the masters and the owners of ships carrying cargoes of wine. The Shipman is dishonest. He has often stolen the wine he is carrying for a merchant, (a chapman such as Chaucer's own father would have been.) When Chaucer calls him a '*good felawe*' he means that he is the very opposite; the irony is a familiar colloquialism today, in such expressions as: 'a fine friend you are'. He certainly allows no delicacy of feeling to act as an impediment to his activities: '*Of nyce conscience took he no keep*'. He seems to have been successful as a ship's captain, although he is illiterate; he knows the coasts he travels very well and is evidently an experienced seaman. No doubt a certain toughness and ruthlessness was an asset in his more nefarious dealings.

It is possible that Chaucer had one particular shipman in mind in this portrait. A ship with the name of the *Magdaleyne* did in fact exist, and there are records of her payment of customs duties in 1379 and 1391. In 1379 her master was a George Cowntree; in 1391, a Peter Risshenden. Several times in the late 1380s ships from Dartmouth, the *Magdaleyne's* home port, were accused of making attacks on other ships. On one occasion Piers Riesselden (Peter Risshenden?) was in charge of a ship which took part in such an affray. Chaucer's Shipman drowned those he took prisoner in such encounters: '*By water he sente hem hoom to every lond.*'

The Shipman's Tale is the story of a merchant who is tricked and duped, but despite its apparently obvious suitability for the Shipman, it was probably not originally designed for him. Lines 12–19 show that the story belongs in a woman's mouth—the Wife of Bath perhaps; the views expressed in these lines could well be her own. But the tale sits well on the Shipman's tongue.

THE WIFE OF BATH

The Wife of Bath is perhaps the most boldly-drawn of Chaucer's characters. She emerges as a vulgar and forceful woman; no lady in the parish dare take precedence over her. She dresses in clothes of expensive quality, bold cut and bold colour. She wears spurs, a broad hat, '*a foot-mantel aboute hir hipes large.*' Her appearance is strikingly in contrast with the Prioress's nervous refinement.

The Wife of Bath has been married five times, but clearly she has never behaved as though she thought herself the humble chattel of any of her husbands. Chaucer whets his audience's curiosity about her early life, and then refuses to say more:

> *Housbondes at chirche dore she hadde fyve,*
> *Withouten oother compaignye in youthe,-*
> *But therof nedeth nat to speke as nowthe.*

Drily, he adds that she has been three times on pilgrimage to Jerusalem, a fact which, were it not for its sharp contrast with what has gone before, would perhaps have indicated that she was a pious woman. She is a caricature of the 'old wife' of the old wives' tale: she knows the '*remedies of love*' and, no doubt, every folk tale and folk remedy for the ills of ordinary people.

The Wife of Bath combines the aggressive self-confidence of one ruled by the planet Mars with the hearty interest in affairs of the heart which belonged, according to the astologers, to those born under the influence of Venus. Chaucer's characterization here is built upon his knowledge of the astrologers' science.

The Wife of Bath tells a story which, as we might expect, deals with a topic close to her own interests: one of the stories in the 'Marriage Group'. She sets out to assert the essential sovereignty of women by telling a version of the common tale of the transformed hag. There were many variants of this story current in Chaucer's day, telling how the hag lies under an enchantment; her would-be husband or lover has to choose between seeing her beautiful at night and hideous in the day-time, or beautiful by day and hideous at night. In Chaucer's version, the hag is not enchanted; she deliberately sets the trap for her husband-to-be, and is thus seen as the dominant partner in the marriage. She makes the rules. The hero, a knight found guilty of rape, has to win his pardon; his captor's queen sets him to find out what women most enjoy. In his search for the answer, he meets the hag, who tells him the answer: women enjoy giving orders and dominating their husbands. The knight conveys this answer to the queen. The hag then claims her forfeit, for she has told him the answer, and he is forced to marry her. The choice with which the hero is presented is between a wife who will be faithful to him, but who will lack all beauty and all grace, and one who is lovely but troublesome. He allows the hag to make the choice for herself. '*Thanne have I gete of yow maistrie*,' she cries in triumph,

30. Venus, in a circle at the top of the page, is shown here with her 'children', typically, lovers and musicians. (Bodleian MS. Rawl. D1220 f. 31ᵛ)

'I have conquered you.' She bestows herself upon him: '*Both fair and good*', as a reward for his submission. The Wife of Bath has not only told a tale altogether in keeping with her interests and of what we know of her past; she appears, too, as an early protagonist for the liberation of women.

THE GILDSMEN

Her social level would probably have been close to that of the five gildsmen who appear to be respected members of their community, even potential leaders of their community as aldermen, but not in the first rank of urban society with the Sergeant of Law and the Merchant. They are sketchily described in the *General Prologue*, and none of them tells a tale. We learn only that they are well-dressed and evidently well-off; they confer a status upon their wives which is reminiscent of the standing of the Wife of Bath herself. Their wives are accustomed to being called 'madame', and to taking first place at those services held on the eves of saints' days, where aldermen's wives took precedence.

31. Among the gildsmen is a '*dyere*' whose trade was the dying of cloth. A dyer is shown here teaching his apprentice his craft. The picture comes from a manuscript of about 1300, which tells the story of the childhood of Christ. The apprentice in this picture is Christ himself. His divinity is shown by a halo; in the apocryphal stories of his childhood, he was said to have been apprenticed to a dyer. (Bodleian MS. Seld. Supra 38 f. 27)

THE WELL-BORN CLERGY

THE PRIORESS

The Prioress's portrait displays Chaucer's use of irony at its most sparkling, and yet at its most gentle. He displays for us her affectations, her social pretensions, her worldliness, her perhaps spurious refinement, yet he does it with so much kindliness that critics have found it difficult to agree about her character; that is, Chaucer leaves us in some doubt as to whether he intends the Prioress to appear as a figure of ridicule or as a woman to be respected for her refinement. The Prioress speaks mincingly, in a French which has never been heard in France, but which, she seems to feel, befits the ladylike front she presents to the world:

> Hire gretteste ooth was but by Seinte Loy; . . .
> And Frenssh she spak ful faire and fetisly
> After the scole of Stratford atte Bowe,
> For Frenssh of Parys was to hire unknowe.

She eats with exquisite neatness:

> At mete wel ytaught was she with alle:
> She leet no morsel from hir lippes falle,
> Ne wette hir fyngres in hir sauce depe;

(This description of the Prioress's fine table manners seems to suggest that the eating-habits of most of her contemporaries were very far from refined; Chaucer remarks on the seemliness of her belching after she has eaten: '*Ful semely after hir mete she raughte*,' not upon the unseemliness of her doing so at all. In such oblique ways does *The Canterbury Tales* colour our picture of the age in which it was written.) The Prioress is tender-hearted, as befits a fine lady; she weeps if she sees a mouse caught in a trap, and she is devoted to the welfare of her lap-dogs. This would have seemed an excessive sensibility in a man, but it is quite in keeping with the Prioress's daintiness, as is her small pursed, rosebud mouth: '*Hir mouth ful small, and therto softe and reed.*'

Her carefully contrived and polished refinement, however, may be interpreted as an aspect of a worldliness which ill-becomes a nun. She wears a bracelet on which is written: 'Love conquers all'. This sentiment could be applied to spiritual as well as to human love, and the ambiguity is deliberate; with his tongue in his cheek, Chaucer plays with words. He mentions the ornament at the end of his description, where it falls most tellingly. First we hear only

32. Simon de Wensley, Rector, had this brass made in his memory in the late 14th century. His feet rest on two lap-dogs which may resemble the Prioress's pets. (BM MS. 75)

that there was an 'A' inscribed on the bracelet: '*On which ther was first write a crowned A*' Then, says Chaucer, there followed the whole legend: '*And after* Amor vincit omnia'. The Prioress's veil of propriety is abruptly lifted. We seem to catch a glimpse of a wordly nun—perhaps a representative of the legion of women put into nunneries because no husband could be found for them, and society had no other use for them; for a moment the Prioress appears a pathetic spinster whose heart would have been far more fully engaged in the life of a merchant's wife than in that of a religious order. But—and here Chaucer leaves us to speculate—the legend may carry only a religious meaning for the Prioress; we may have misjudged her.

Certainly, the Prioress had no business to be going on pilgrimage at all. Her vows should have bound her to stay in her convent. Her lap-dogs and her bracelet were not the proper accoutrements of a nun, nor, probably, should her wimple have been fancifully pleated. Her table-manners closely resemble those described in the *Roman de la Rose* as a model for fashionable young ladies to emulate.

The Prioress's Tale is brief. She tells one of the many legends about the miracles performed by the Blessed Virgin Mary, which were in common circulation; at least twenty-seven similar stories have been identified. In medieval lore there are many accounts of the murder of Christian children by Jews. In a world where almost everyone was, at least nominally, a Christian, those who held another faith formed a minority whose members were regarded with great suspicion and hostility, and the Jews were often blamed for crimes they had not committed. The stories of Hugh of Lincoln and of William of Norwich are perhaps among the best-known. The Prioress describes in elegant and graceful verse the story of the martyrdom of such a child, who was said to have sung a hymn to the Virgin after his throat had been cut. The style and the subject-matter are neatly matched to the teller, whose 'refinement' dictates their shape.

THE MONK

The Monk, Daun Piers, is well-born, the Prioress's social counterpart. He is a suitable candidate for the office of Abbot, which was generally reserved for those born into an appropriate social class rather than for those whose chief qualification was their piety. His pleasures and his habits reflect this social background. Hunting, an appreciation of well-bred dogs and fine horses and an enjoyment of the best in food and clothing would be perfectly proper to the Monk had he not been a member of a religious order. He is an '*outridere*', that is, a monk who was given the task of taking care of his monastery's estates. He would therefore necessarily spend more time outside the walls of the monastery than was normally considered good for a monk's spiritual health; in the course of carrying out his duties he would have mingled professionally and socially with the local landowners and farmers. His gifts qualify him to be an administrator, to take excellent care of the material possessions of the monastery, but they would have made him quite unfitted to undertake the pastoral care of monks or to watch over their spiritual welfare. In fact, he feels that the more stringent and restrictive details of the rule laid down by St Benedict are simply out of date.

In Chaucer's day many monasteries had grown wealthy on the gifts of pious laymen, who gave their goods and lands to the Church as an act of charity. The monasteries were inevitably changed by the possession of great wealth. It would be difficult for the monks of such abbeys to live lives of holy poverty amidst a rich store of possessions but comparatively wordly monks such as Daun Piers had a place in their administration.

The Host taunts the Monk good-naturedly about his prosperous appearance; Daun Piers takes the jesting well, with dignity. He offers to tell a tale very different from that hunting story which the company might have expected.

The Monk tells the story of the fall of a number of famous men; Chaucer presumably drew his general scheme from Boccaccio's work; *De Casibus Virorum Illustrium*—he acknowledges the borrowing in his own subtitle. But the form, and the idea of telling a series of anecdotes on a common theme, is familiar in medieval writing: Chaucer uses it himself in *The Legend of Good Women*. The Monk would perhaps have found that such convivial stories went down well with his friends among the farming gentry.

THE NUN'S PRIEST: A SHADOWY FIGURE

This character, who is one of the three priests who accompany the Prioress and her Nun, is merely a name in the *General Prologue*. He may have been one of the nuns' chaplains, or he and his fellow priests may be riding with the nuns in order to give them their protection. His tale is the well-known story of Chantecleer and Pertelote, the vain cock and the hen, and the wily fox. It is a moral tale, a fable like those of the Greek writer of fables, Aesop, in which the cock's pride and vainglory bring about his downfall; it is thus well suited to be told by a priest, who would employ such *exempla* or illustrative stories, to press home a point in a sermon by pointing to an example of the fate that might befall the victim of such a vice. Like the Pardoner, the Nun's Priest may have had occasion to preach himself, though not all medieval priests were preachers. But he would certainly have heard sermons, and have been familiar with the device he uses here.

A LATE ARRIVAL

The Canon and his Yeoman come panting after the main company of pilgrims, when the journey is already nearing its end. They are hot and breathless because of their efforts to catch up. After the Second Nun has told her tale, when the pilgrims are near Boughton-under-Blee, a black cloaked figure on a sweating horse overtakes the pilgrims:

> *His hakeney, that was al pomely grys,*
> *So swatte that it wonder was to see;*
> *It semed as he had priked miles three.*

This is the Canon's Yeoman, who claims that it is he who has encouraged his master to hurry, because he saw the pilgrims leaving the Inn and was attracted by their evident merriment and jollity into thinking that they would be good company. The Yeoman is the more talkative of the two newcomers. He begins to chatter about his master's doings, and the Canon, embarrassed, draws away from the company, leaving the Yeoman to enjoy the centre of attention and to tell his tale.

There has been a good deal of discussion as to whether Chaucer deliberately introduces the Canon's Yeoman at this point, in order to add a new face to the company, or whether he and his tale are no more than an afterthought. Chaucer might have thought of him later and still introduced him into *The General Prologue* amongst the rest of the company. His arrival therefore seems more likely to be a literary device intended to introduce a new element into the pattern of the relationships which have already been established among the pilgrims.

The Canon's Yeoman's Tale is largely an autobiography. He begins with his apprenticeship to a master of alchemy, who is also a canon, and then he goes on to tell a series of anecdotes about his life in the service of another, different canon. This format provides a frame for a varied collection of anecdotes into which Chaucer was able to introduce fragments of his own knowledge about alchemy. No source has been found; the story is simply a vehicle for a number of assorted items of narrative. The Canon's Yeoman tells a racy, gossipy tale whose very hotch-potch quality is eminently suited to his character.

Not all of Chaucer's pilgrims have come on pilgrimage alone. The Wife of Bath, the Clerk of Oxenford, the Shipman, for example, travel by themselves, but the Knight has with him his son the Squire and his Yeoman; the Sergeant of Law is accompanied by the Franklin; the Gildsmen travel with their Cook; the Summoner and the Pardoner ride together. As on a modern coach tour, the travelling companions come in twos or threes or singly. (But Chaucer includes no families in his group.) Chaucer thus adds variety and interest and an additional verisimilitude to his portrayal of a company of people thrown together for a few days on a common journey.

His pilgrims are far from being a mere collection of representative members of the society he knew: one monk, one knight, one miller, and so on. Some may have been portraits of real people; others are mere types, but all are drawn with a quick eye for detail which suggests that Chaucer, like a modern novelist, would have drawn directly on his own observation of people.

THE FIRST ENGLISH NOVEL?

Setting aside the fact that Chaucer wrote in verse, while the modern novel is essentially a prose form, how far does this apparent jumble of tales and tellers add up to something which resembles the modern novel? Certainly, Chaucer's gift for narrative, and for pointed and observant description, would serve a modern novelist well. The device of using a teller to tell his story is not uncommon in modern novels, but it would not come naturally to a modern novelist to try to link a series of unrelated short stories in quite the way that Chaucer does. Equally, the use of familiar or well-known stories would not seem appropriate to most modern novelists.

But Chaucer's *Canterbury Tales* contrasts with the majority of his other works. Where the works which were most admired by his contemporaries and immediate successors owe a good deal to the example of the poems which Chaucer took as his models, in particular those of France, *The Canterbury Tales* has a format which is especially Chaucer's. His characters are lively, complex, fallible human beings, who interact with each other in something of the way in which characters in a modern novel behave. Chaucer's people are presented in close-up: it is in his portrayal of people, rather than in the theme, subject-matter, form or style of *The Canterbury Tales*, that Chaucer writes like a novelist.

The likeness of Chaucer's *Canterbury Tales* to a modern novel is slight but the poem is the nearest the writers of the 14th century came to anticipating a form of composition which was not to become popular until the 18th century. Chaucer's work can in no direct sense be considered an ancestor of the modern novel; but Chaucer himself seems to have the gifts of a novelist, had he been born in another age where he could have made use of them.

All quotations are from Geoffrey Chaucer *Works* Ed. F. W. Robinson (O.U.P. 1957, 1974).

7

Chaucer's Language and Rhetoric

Medieval writers saw themselves as craftsmen, as skilled workers who possessed a command of the technicalities of their trade. Chaucer was familiar with certain rules and principles of composition. That is not to say that he necessarily followed a whole manual of rules (although such manuals on 'the art of poetry' did exist) but he would have had standards of excellence, and he could probably have given his reasons for choosing one word rather than another. In the poetry he had read he found models of good writing with which to compare his own compositions. Chaucer would have seen no merit in expressing his ideas spontaneously, with no concern for the appropriateness of the words, the style and the form in which he couched what he wanted to say. What he wrote stands up to close analysis because he composed with care and deliberation. That does not make Chaucer's writing in any way mechanical or laboured—he is sufficiently master of his medium to be able to break the rules boldly when it suits his purposes—but it means that his writing repays the reader for the trouble of coming back to it again and again.

33. This late-15th century illustration, from the *Grammatica Nova*, shows a schoolmaster—or perhaps a tutor—instructing schoolboys in the 'new grammar'. Master and boys have books before them, but there are no other aids to teaching. Without pictures, filmstrips, television, tape-recorders or even blackboards or chalk, the schoolrooms of the Middle Ages were austere places where the only stimulus to learning came from the master himself; discipline was usually severe; if a boy was unwilling, or unable to learn, he was beaten. It was believed that moral and intellectual training should go together. (BM PB 25)

Three essential elements in the use of language had been distinguished from each other long before Chaucer's time, by the writers of Classical Greece and Rome. Grammar was the art of speaking and writing correctly; logic, the technique of arguing reasonably and clearly, and rhetoric, the art of persuasion. The study of grammar, logic and rhetoric made up the three foundation studies of medieval students. In all, there were seven liberal arts. These three were known collectively as the *trivium*; the other four, arithmetic, geometry, music, astronomy, as the *quadrivium*.

The study of grammar involved far more than the mere analysis of the structure of language; as well as learning to identify nouns and verbs, prepositions and conjunctions and the rest of the eight parts of speech, the pupil studied common errors, etymology (or the supposed derivations of difficult words), certain stylistic devices, prose and verse, history and fable. It is unlikely that the average student was equally well-grounded in every aspect of the study of grammar. For most men of average education the study of grammar in the schools meant the patient translation of passages from Latin authors, with a detailed study of their technical skills. This is probably the sense in which Chaucer studied grammar. There were textbooks of grammar, by two late-Roman grammarians, Priscian and Donatus, which laid down a systematic scheme of study, and provided examples drawn from Classical writers.

In studying logic, certain of Aristotle's works had long been the accepted textbooks. In the 6th century Boethius wrote commentaries on Aristotle, and original treatises of his own on specific problems. During the 12th century a number of additional works of Aristotle had begun to circulate, and the possibilities of formal logic had been greatly expanded and explored. The function of logic was to teach a scholar to argue clearly and convincingly. It had become, by Chaucer's time, an immensely technical skill; the ordinary man would have found the logicians' arguments as incomprehensible as a modern layman would find the specialized language of certain sciences, or the formulae of higher mathematics. As we have seen, Chaucer's Clerk of Oxenford, who is a scholar, has studied logic:

> *A Clerk ther was of Oxenford also*
> *That unto logyk hadde long ygo.*

He would rather have the books of '*Aristotle and his philosophie*' than fine clothes. He would have learned to match his wits in formal disputations against his fellow-students on such problems as these:

'If a tree burns it is consumed. How, then can Moses have seen a burning bush which was not burnt up? If a branch is cut from a tree, it does not flower and fruit. Therefore it seems that Aaron's rod cannot have budded'. Thomas Aquinas, the 13th century philosopher, had compiled handbooks of formal disputation in which the proper arguments to be used in settling any issue were set out in order, together with the master's resolution of the problem.

Language can be used as a vehicle of argument. It may equally become a vehicle of persuasion. An argument may convince the reason without involving the emotions. One function of rhetoric is to overwhelm the reader's feelings in such a way that he accepts what he is being told without allowing his reason to examine it coldly. The following simple example illustrates the difference between a logical argument and another, which is rhetorically expressed:

> Only one set of fingerprints was found in the room where the murder was committed.
> The fingerprints are those of Mr. Brown.
> Mr. Brown must therefore be the murderer.

> John Brown is known to you all as a reliable friend, a generous husband and a devoted father. His war record shows him to be a man of unusual courage. Can you bring yourselves to believe that such slight and circumstantial evidence as the finding of Mr. Brown's fingerprints in a room in any way suggests that he is capable of committing this dreadful crime?

But rhetoric possessed as many technical terms, and as complex a set of rules and principles as logic. Chaucer's Host, Harry Bailly, persuades the Clerk to tell his tale in a speech which mentions several of the commoner technical terms of rhetoric:

> *Teele us som murie thyng of aventures.*
> *Youre termes, youre colours and your figures,*
> *Keepe hem in stoor til so be that ye endite*
> *Heigh style, as whan that men to kynges write.*
> *Speketh so pleyn at this time, we yow preye,*
> *That we may understonde what ye seye.*

'*Colours*' are rhetorical ornaments, '*figures*' figures of speech, such as metaphor, simile, personification, '*termes*', elegant phrases.

The Host begs the Clerk to keep such fancy decorations for writing to kings and other important persons in the 'high style' appropriate to the task (the 'art of letter-writing' laid down the rules in such matters). The Clerk is asked to tell his story plainly; evidently those skilled in the rhetorical art sometimes made such heavy-handed use of its teachings that no one but a fellow-rhetorician could understand their flowery speeches.

The formal study of rhetoric in the universities was barely established in Chaucer's day, but there had been a lively interest in rhetorical methods of argument for centuries, and rhetorical theories of style had been taught as part of the study of grammar. Of the textbooks, Cicero's *On Invention* dealt with methods of argument, especially with ways of finding material or evidence to make an argument more convincing. The *Herennian Rhetoric*—which was then also believed to be by Cicero—taught a wider range of technical skills. The best textbook of all was Quintilian's *Institutes of Oratory*, but this was little-known until the later Middle Ages; it was a comprehensive manual of the skills of language, beginning with the teaching of the elements of grammar to the young boy, and explaining how he should be introduced to the higher study of rhetoric in all its aspects.

In Classical times, rhetoric had grown three branches: it was used in public-speaking (in what we might call political speeches), in the law-courts, and for making formal speeches in praise of important men. It taught the elementary principles of composition —how a speech must have a beginning, a middle and an end. It explained the methods of persuasion: the use of a number of examples and illustrations to make the point in hand seem more acceptable; most people will tend to feel that if A, B, C, D and E are shown to be true, then F is to be believed, too. The orator was taught to flatter and cajole his audience, to keep their interest by constantly varying his approach. Some of these aspects of rhetoric were of less interest to the people of the Middle Ages, where formal public-speaking of any kind was almost unheard-of, except for the preaching of sermons. Medieval writers borrowed from Classical rhetoric chiefly the range of stylistic devices which were touched on in the study of grammar.

Three separate branches of the medieval art of rhetoric leave some traces in Chaucer's poems. The 'art of letter-writing' has already been mentioned. It developed in the 11th century to provide the clerks who wrote the letters of popes and kings with a scheme of composition. The new art taught the clerks to avoid the heavy-handed elaborations with which their letters had been laden, in favour of a simpler and more elegant style, whose sentences came to graceful conclusions like the cadences in music. The third of the arts to develop from Classical rhetoric in medieval times was the 'art of preaching'. The textbooks of this art date for the most part from the middle of the 13th century or later; the preacher was taught to take a text from the Bible as his theme, and to divide and subdivide the aspects of the theme until he had exhausted his subject. He was encouraged to illustrate what he was saying by telling apt little stories which made his rather abstract arguments seem more concrete and colourful to his less well-educated listeners. These *exempla* provide more than one of Chaucer's ecclesiastical characters with material for their stories, as we have seen.

34. The bishop who is preaching here has a very mixed audience. Above his head a heavenly audience listens with the earthly audience below. Clergy and laity are both represented, young and old. In fact it is probable that many preachers addressed themselves to audiences which consisted chiefly of one kind of listener. In the handbooks on the 'art of preaching' there is advice about the kind of sermon which is likely to be most effective when it is delivered to each type of audience: there are sermons for clerks, sermons for scholars, sermons for monks, sermons for merchants, knights, widows, young girls, even sermons for kings and princes. The preacher was by no means always a bishop. But the artist here has tried to represent in one picture the whole body of Christian people listening to a preacher. (BM MS. Royal 8 G III f. 2)

The second of the medieval rhetorical arts is the one which concerns us most closely: the 'art of poetry'. During the 12th century the writing of poems in Latin and French—as well as in other languages—reawakened an active interest in the art of poetical composition: Geoffrey of Vinsauf's book, *The New Poetry*, became a popular manual. Chaucer certainly knew of it, although there is no direct evidence that he had read the work itself. In *The House of Fame* he mentions the '*art poetical*', and in *The Nun's Priest's Tale*, when the fox captures Chauntecleer, Chaucer makes a joke of the solemn poet who would follow Geoffrey of Vinsauf's manual here and rage against the day on which such a tragic event took place:

> *O Gaufred, deere maister soverayn*
> *That when thy worthy kyng Richard was slayn*
> *With shot, compleynedst his deeth so soore,*
> *Why ne hadde I now thy sentence and thy loore,*
> *The Friday for to chide as diden ye?*

'If only,' cries Chaucer, 'I knew how to chastise that evil day as roundly as you did!' In *Troilus and Criseyde*, too, Chaucer quotes Geoffrey.

This, then, was the educational background to the formal study of the art of writing in Chaucer's day. In certain respects it could be a more exacting and detailed training than that to which a modern writer might submit himself. Although Chaucer learned his own craft chiefly by studying examples and by imitation of other poets' work and probably not from a textbook, he would not have appreciated the merits of poetry written without form, or without formal technical skill, however fine and fresh its ideas. He would barely have understood what we mean by 'creative writing'. Chaucer's own knowledge must have been of a different kind to that of the Latin scholars of the universities, with their intensive study of logic, and their complex technicality of method. He was an educated man with a serious and informed interest in the culture of his time. He was not an academic or a scholar, yet his writing is very far from being unstudied or careless. Chaucer had developed criteria of taste and a sound background knowledge of the opinions about literature which were current among his friends at court and in the civil service.

In Renaissance times, an educated man with an active intellectual curiosity could achieve a fair grasp of every subject, including current affairs. Shakespeare displays a knowledge of a number of arts and professions which has led critics to claim that he must himself have been a lawyer, a sailor, or a soldier, for example. Chaucer possessed an exactly similar command of the learning and culture of his day. This pleasure is beyond the reach of modern man. The range and depth of human knowledge has so much increased and expanded that no single human mind can comprehend the encyclopedaic range of knowledge. It has become necessary to specialize. There is, too, a modern mistrust of the opinions of the dilettante, the man who dips into fields outside his own special competence, and dares to pronounce opinions on subjects in which he is no expert. This may deprive us of another Chaucer.

CHAUCER'S LANGUAGE

The scholarly circles of the 14th century still revolved almost exclusively around the study of works in Latin. Chaucer wrote in English. In two respects this has some significance. Even Milton, three hundred years later, felt that *Paradise Lost* would have been a greater poem if he had written it in Latin. Latin had a certain prestige, and serious works about important or elevated subjects were felt to be most appropriately written in Latin. Even if we take it that Chaucer would have wished to make no such claims for the majority of his poems, if he had been born half a century earlier, we should have expected him to write not in English, but in French.

When William the Conqueror took possession of England in 1066, his Normans brought their language with them. Administrative and legal documents were written in Latin or in Norman French until the 14th century; then the English language which is the ancestor of modern English began to assert itself. (In 1362 it was decreed by Act of Parliament that French was no longer to be used in the law-courts.) The language of the Anglo-Saxon England which William had conquered had never died out among ordinary people, but the middle and upper classes had spoken French in preference to English. Chaucer's English has some claim to be viewed as a hybrid language, in which a number of words and usages of French origin have enriched the vocabulary of Old English and modified its structure. It is important to realize that he wrote in the ordinary London speech of his time, and not in a new language artificially created by himself. He does introduce words which were not in common use in London, odd provincialisms for example, and sometimes the search for a rhyme leads him to choose an unfamiliar word. But it is in the *Treatise on the Astrolabe* that we find the earliest reference to 'King's English' and that is the language which Chaucer quite consciously used.

There has, however, never been a single English language; Chaucer's East Midland dialect is perhaps the closest to modern English, because it was the language of the capital city, and so it exerted a strong influence on the later development of the language. But among contemporary writers, Langland, the author of *Piers Plowman*, wrote in a version of the South Midland dialect, and the anonymous author of *Sir Gawain and the Green Knight* wrote in a North-West Midland dialect. Chaucer himself remarks, at the end of *Troilus and Criseyde*, on the variety of the English dialects:

> *An for ther is so gret diversite*
> *In Englissh and in writyng of oure tonge*
> *So prey I God that non miswrite the . . .*

and:

> *Ye knowe ek that in forme of speche is chaunge.*

Chaucer's English has certain characteristics which it owes to its origins in Old English. Old English was an inflected language, like Latin, or modern German, or Russian. That is, the endings of many words change to match their grammatical place and function. Some of this complexity had disappeared by Chaucer's time. The ending 's' or 'es' in the plural and in the possessive, (which we still use with an apostrophe to precede it, as in 'Chaucer's poems') survived. Certain plurals were formed without a special ending, as they still are (*deer*, *sheep*). Some nouns formed their plural by a change of vowel (*men*, *geese*), as they still do. Others had a plural in -en (*eyen*, *hosen*, *pesen*, *been*). Traces of the Old English noun- and verb-forms, then, still survive, but they were more numerous in Chaucer's day.

The past participle often has the prefix 'y': *y-sungen*, *y-taught*. Some verbs: 'to be', 'to go', 'to have', 'to do', 'to will', are exceptionally irregular—as they are in modern English, and in numerous other languages. So fundamental are these verbs to language that it seems that they are early hammered out of shape by sheer hard usage. In the verb 'to go' the forms *goon*, *yede*, *wente*, are all found; in the past tense of *doon*, we find *dide*; in the verb 'to be' the present forms *am*, *art*, *is*, with the plural *been*, *be*, yield, in the past tense, *was*, *were*, *were(n)*. There are certain misleading differences. When Chaucer wants to say 'was not' or 'is not' the form he uses is *ne was* or *ne is*, which elides smoothly into *nas* or *nis*. In '*There nas no traitor but Judas hymselve*', he is merely reinforcing his negative and making it more emphatic when he puts two negatives together, rather as in modern French or in some regional dialects of English.

Chaucer's verse has caused a great deal of controversy. In order to follow the rhythm as he intends it, it is necessary to remember that he pronounced the final 'e' except before an initial vowel or a silent 'h'. His basic line is that in which Shakespeare wrote, and of which blank verse is composed: the iambic pentameter. English accommodates itself naturally and comfortably to this line of five feet, with a rhythm of alternating unstressed and stressed syllables.

Fŭl stréit(e) | *ўteýd* ‖ *ănd shóes* | *fŭl móyst(e)* | *ănd néw(e).*

Chaucer, like any other poet who employs this kind of line with skill and facility, often varies it to avoid monotony. He reverses his iambic feet into trochaic feet (⌣); sometimes he omits the unaccented syllable with which a line begins. His very variety and flexibility has made it impossible for his editors to be certain that they have read his intentions correctly. The above example, suggested by R. W. V. Eliott as an instance of a line which has perfect regularity, on the basis of what he calls '*semantically justifiable stress*'[1] might well be queried by other scholars, as he acknowledges. One of the major difficulties in studying a language, or a form of language, which is no longer actually spoken, is to know how it sounded.

CHAUCER AND HIS CONTEMPORARIES

Chaucer may stand head and shoulders above his contemporaries as a poet, but he did not write in a position of splendid isolation. Not only his special qualities, but also his place within the literary tradition of his own day, become clear only when he is compared with contemporary writers. A short quotation from *Sir Gawain* will serve to show how strongly Northern English contrasts with that of Chaucer's London, and how the old alliterative verse form differs from Chaucer's rhyming verse:

Wel gay was this gome gered in grene
and the here of his hed of his hors suete:
Fayre fannand fax umbefoldes his schulderes.
As much berd as a busk over his brest henges,
that myth his highlich here that of his hed reches

Was evesed al umbetorne abof his elbowes,
That half his armes ther under were halched in the wyse
Of kynges capados that closes his swyre[2]

Yes, garbed all in green was the gallant rider.
His hair, like his horse in hue, hung light
Clustering in curls like a cloak round his shoulders,
And a great bushy beard on his breast flowing down,
With the lovely locks hanging loose from his head,
Was shorn below the shoulder, sheared right round,
So that half his arms were under the encircling hair.
Covered as by a King's cape, that closes at the neck.[3]

William Langland's verse, too, is alliterative.

In a somer seasoun, when softe was the sonne,
I shope me into shroudes, as I a shep were,
On abite as an heremite, unholy of werkes,
Wente forth in the world wondres to here,
And saw many selles and selcouthe thynges.
Ac on a May Mornyng on Malvern hulles,
Ne biful for to slepe, for werynesse of walkyng;
And yn a launde as I lay, lened I and slepte,
And merveylousliche me mette, as I may telle.[4]

One summer season, when the sun was warm, I rigged myself
out in shabby woollen clothes, as if I were a shepherd; and in the
garb of an easy-living hermit I set out to roam far and wide
through the world, hoping to hear of marvels. But on a morning
in May among the Malvern Hills, a strange thing happened to
me, as though by magic. For I was tired out by my wanderings,
and as I lay down to rest under a broad bank by the side of a
stream and leaned over gazing into the water, it sounded so
pleasant that I fell asleep.[5]

   William Langland's life is something of a mystery; he was a
cleric but comparatively little is known of his career. There is no
reason to think that Chaucer had read his work. His poem describes
a vision, or rather, a series of dreams. The dreamer is a vagrant who
writes in the first person, but there is no reason to suppose that
Langland is really telling us about himself. His narrator is more
probably a mere creation, a convenient teller of the tale. Sometimes
he preaches to his readers; sometimes he tells the story without

comment, only indirectly telling us what he thinks about the world he sees around him.

If Chaucer's English can be said to stand on the boundary between modern English and that older language which we must translate before we can understand it, then *Sir Gawain* clearly lies on the far side of that line. It remains open to question how far *Sir Gawain* and *Piers Plowman* should be regarded as transitional works, steps on the path by which English literature came to form its own distinctive character. They are English in their language and style to a degree that Chaucer's works, under the influence of his admiration for French poetry, are not. To call them 'pre-literary' is perhaps to imply that poetry composed without the benefit of the study of a self-consciously literary mode of composi-tion, is, in some sense, barely to be considered literature at all. Both these poems show a number of influences upon their style and subject-matter; they are far from being artless works. Yet they are less sophisticated than Chaucer's courtly poetry. Chaucer, however, could have written in French; it is his choice of English as a literary vehicle of expression which shows how far the language had already progressed, in the hands of near contemporaries, towards being a fit instrument for poetical expression of a variety of kinds, and of a high level of technical expertise. Langland is involved in his subject in a way that Chaucer is not; Chaucer's capacity for irony arises from his detachment; Langland cares deeply about the abuses he attacks, and on occasion he rants and rages against the world like a popular preacher. It is difficult, in reading the Middle English sermons of which copies have survived, to feel the force with which they might have struck an audience which actually heard them. We cannot know whether the preacher carefully composed his sermon in his study before standing up to preach, or whether he collected his ideas together only in his mind, and then let them flow as mood or inspiration took him, writing out a polished version later so that the sermon might be read by others, and thus enlarge the sphere of its edifying influence. In exhorting men to virtue the preacher had scope for eloquence; but in fulminating against vices and cor-ruption he had the opportunity to terrify his listeners with accounts of the fate which awaited the unrepentant sinner in hell. There seems to have been no fear of blunting the susceptibility of the audience by repeated emphasis of these horrors; sermon after sermon carries the same burden. Perhaps the majority of men heard sermons infrequently enough for this to constitute no great prob-lem. Langland is certainly under no restraint in his attempts to communicate his own concern to his readers. Chaucer's choice of words and expressions is subject to a far more subtle system of checks and balances.

John Gower, a friend of Chaucer and fellow-Londoner, wrote a *Lover's Confession* in which he sets out to discuss the subject of courtly love under a series of headings provided by the Seven Deadly Sins. He illustrates his arguments and draws his morals by telling appropriate stories, (taken from a similar range of sources to Chaucer's). The subject-matter is divided and subdivided, as was customary, especially in the preaching of sermons at that time. Wrath, for example, is divided into Melancholy, Chiding, Hatred, Quarrelsomeness and Murder, Violence and War; Sloth is divided into Delay, Indecisiveness, Forgetfulness, Negligence, Idleness, Somnolence, Obstinacy, Despondency. For each form of each vice there is an illustrative story.

The language of John Gower may again be compared with that of Chaucer; because both wrote in the same dialect, the similarities are closer than those between the language in which *Piers Plowman* is written and the language of Chaucer's London:

> *I may nought strecche up to the heven*
> *Min hond, ne setten al in even*
> *This world, whiche ever is in balaunce;*
> *It stant nought in my suffisaunce*
> *So greate thinges to compasse.*
> *But I mote lette it over passe*
> *And treaten upon other thinges.*[6]

> *I may not stretch up to the heavens*
> *This hand of mine, nor set at evens*
> *This world that wavers on the scales;*
> *Little my slender power avails*
> *To compass things so great and high;*
> *So I must let them pass me by,*
> *And find new matters to recite.*[7]

Chaucer, then, did not write in a dialect which was in common use all over England, nor was his poetry couched in a form which would have been equally pleasing to every English audience. But he wrote in English, and he chose the technically difficult and complex art-form of poetry. His love of making lists (of names, of things, of places), his delight in digression and amplification, in drawing portraits, in playing games with words, are all indications of his familiarity with the graces which were considered appropriate to poetical composition in his day. Both Chaucer's language and Chaucer's rhetoric contribute to the characteristic flavour of his writing; it is a testimony to the flexibility and comparative sophistication of the language in which Chaucer chose to write that he was able to do so much.

[1] R. W. V. Elliot *Chaucer's English* (Deutsch, 1974) p. 24 [2] R. A. Waldron (Ed.) *Sir Gawain and the Green Knight* (Ed. Arnold, 1970) p. 38 [3] B. Stone (Ed.) *Sir Gawain and the Green Knight* (Penguin, 1970) p. 30 [4] W. Langland *Piers Plowman* ed. E. Salter and D. Pearsall (Ed. Arnold, 1967) I lines 1–9 [5] W. Langland *Piers Plowman* trns. into Mod. English by J. F. Goodridge (Penguin, 1970) p. 63 [6] J. Gower *Confessio Amantis* ed. H. Morley, 1889, p. 48 [7] J. Gower *Confessio Amantis* trns. into Mod. English by T. Tiller (Penguin,) p. 44.

8

The Chaucerian Voice

Chaucer's sense of the ridiculous leads him to laugh at human failings—often quite gently, or in a spirit of affectionate teasing; sometimes he pokes a character in the ribs with a more fiercely accusing finger. Among Chaucer's poems, *The Canterbury Tales*, in particular, have appealed to people in different periods for different reasons. He has not always been enjoyed for his irony. In the 15th century he was respected as a *'noble and grete philosopher'*[1] his poems were viewed as models of the court poetry written for the pleasure of a substantially aristocratic audience. Chaucer therefore had considerable dignity and stature in the eyes of his critics. But Sir Philip Sidney, writing in the 16th century, already saw him, for all his greatness, as a poet of the distant past:

> *I know not whether to marvel more, either that he in that misty time could see so clearly, or that we in this clear age walk so stumblingly after him.*[2]

Dryden, a century later still, saw him as a poet who *'followed Nature everywhere, but was never so bold as to go beyond her'*[3], as a poet whose art and artifice were subordinated to his realism, who described real life closely and went no further. Hazlitt, at the beginning of the 19th century, regarded Chaucer as a man of the world:

> *Chaucer's intercourse with the busy world, and collision with the actual passions and conflicting interests of others, seemed to brace the sinews of his understanding.*[4]

Whether we feel that his characters have a richness and roundness which reflects his own warm humanity, or that he was simply a poet who handled the poetical conventions of his day with exceptional skill and expertise, Chaucer is still capable of surprising. E. T. Donaldson has said that it is a quality of most great poetry to be *'always open to reinterpretation.'*[5] It is a measure of Chaucer's success as an ironist that it is not always obvious whether he intends to be funny, to be cruel or to be serious.

H

Sir Philip Sidney's remark should bring us up short. Chaucer's language may seem to have, on first acquaintance, an appearance of rough-hewn simplicity. The better we understand his language and his culture, the more evidence of his artistry we find beneath the surface of his words. Similarly, we should be on our guard against regarding Chaucer as a simple soul who belongs to an age of men who were unsophisticated or naive, in comparison with modern people. Sidney was surprised that '*in that misty time*' Chaucer '*could see so clearly*'. But Chaucer's times were of course as brilliantly clear and immediate to him as today's events are to us, and he was, as we have seen, a man of the world with a great deal of sophistication and a fine mind. He would have held his own today in any company with his shrewd and piercing, if not unkindly, wit.

Perhaps Chaucer's irony and his humour reveal the man himself. Perhaps they show him to us in disguise. Like Jane Austen's humour, Chaucer's irony does not always make itself obvious on a first reading; it is subtle stuff. 'Chaucer' himself is one of the characters in his own group of pilgrims, and he portrays himself, dryly, as something of a fool. When the Host invites him to tell his tale, he replies that he knows only one tale, and that an old one:

> '*Hooste*', *quod I*, '*ne beth nat yvele apayd,*
> *For oother tale certes kan I noon,*
> *But of a rym I lerned long agoon*'.

Chaucer's first attempt at a story, *The Tale of Sir Topas*, is a confidently executed burlesque of an Old English romance; perhaps Chaucer's chief pleasure is in mocking the Flemings who pretended to knighthood, despite their urban background and their lowliness of birth. Chaucer's double satire, literary and social is matched by a third irony: the tale is deliberately told in an inept manner, so that the host has to interrupt him when he can bear it no longer. 'You are wasting time!' he cries: '*Thou doost noght elles but despendest tyme*'. He begs him to tell a prose story, or at least to say something: '*In which ther be som murthe or som doctryne*'. Chaucer promises to '*telle a littel thyng in prose*', that is, *The Tale of Melibee*, which, with heavy irony, he goes on to tell at great length. Chaucer mocks himself, then, very obviously, in his portrayal of his own character in *The Canterbury Tales*, and in the opening of *The House of Fame*, where he disclaims his own skill (a common medieval practice).

His irony can be gentle and understated, mild, yet penetrating. In the *General Prologue* we have already met a number of pilgrims whose characters have been delineated with a few deft strokes. Irony gains a good deal of its pointedness from the economy with which it is used (just as a joke is much funnier if the punch-line takes the listener by surprise). Chaucer understood this principle very well; the Cook who accompanies the Haberdasshere, the Carpenter, the Webbe, the Dyere and the Tapicer (the five 'gildsmen') is an excellent cook; he can '*rooste, and sethe, and broille, and frye/Maken mortreux, and wel bake a pye.*' But Chaucer comments wrily that he has a running sore on his leg; he brings home the remark by immediately mentioning the Cook's skill in making the original of modern blancmange, a white stew of poultry with rice, almonds, sugar and eggs.

> *But greet harm was it, as it thoughte me,*
> *That on his shyne a mormal hadde he.*
> *For blankmanger, that made he with the beste.*

Even a medieval audience, unaccustomed to modern standards of hygiene, must have felt a tremor of revulsion at this.

Chaucer's irony works like yeast through the writing of *The Canterbury Tales*, enlivening every part with humour. Chaucer uses irony because his chief purpose is to entertain, and because no rhetorical device so flatters an audience as the suggestion that they have a wit and penetration which enables them to see through the characters which are paraded before them. Chaucer keeps his listeners' interest by giving them a racy account of the failings of his characters, as well as letting them in on the poet's private knowledge. He thus heightens the plain appeal of a series of good stories well told, with an extra spiciness.

These, then, are general characteristics of Chaucer's irony; but students of Chaucer have attempted to distinguish a number of different kinds of irony in his writings, and to define his notion of irony much more precisely. A writer who employs irony is being in some way indirect in his statements; he may say the opposite of what he means, while giving his reader a hint of his real intentions which may amount to a mere nudge or to a broad wink. He may pretend not to have noticed some detail, and to be entirely caught up in describing something else; but his pointed omission of any reference to an obvious item of description may still draw the reader's attention in that direction. He may describe a comparable figure or a similar event, in order to show up certain features of his real subject by comparison. A good deal of what is nowadays colloquially called 'sarcasm' should more properly come under the heading of 'irony';

true sarcasm has a biting edge to it which may be altogether absent from gentler or more subtle forms of irony.

Chaucer's critics have made out cases for his use of at least five kinds of irony. A list of examples of Chaucer's use of a number of different kinds of irony proves only the critic's skill in finding and identifying them; it cannot prove that Chaucer himself was conscious that he was employing different varieties of irony, although we may be sure than when he gives an ironic twist to a description he is well aware of its general effect. We can only suggest what may have been his larger intentions.

Two preliminary remarks may safely be made. Irony demands a 'double audience'. That is, it must be possible to distinguish an audience of those 'in the know' from those who are not. In *The Canterbury Tales* the pilgrims themselves 'know' about each other what Chaucer allows them to tell each other, and what they can observe. But *we* know what Chaucer tells us in an occasional 'aside' to his audience. 'Asides' are not part of the dramatic conventions of our day, although Robert Bolt uses a commentator to address the audience in *A Man for All Seasons* and the literary device of a narrator is widely used in novels, films and television. There can be no irony where there is no one to savour the possession of privileged information, or to suffer because of the lack of it.

Secondly, we might distinguish between the smaller ironies of Chaucer's detailed descriptions, and the larger implications of his use of irony. It is possible, by setting together two unperceived contradictions, to appear to turn the world upside-down. We see Chaucer's characters, such as the Wife of Bath, as ordinary human beings. But in the eyes of Chaucer's contemporaries, she is also a being whose behaviour is governed by the great cosmic influences of the stars. The Knight, though a great deal flatter as a character, displays the ideal virtues of knighthood as they ought to have been practised in the daily life of knights of Chaucer's time; but he also stands for the 'soldier of Christ'. For each of Chaucer's characters it is possible to construct a place in an otherwordly scheme of things, where the pilgrims stand for eternal qualities. This double meaning is not immediately self-evident to a modern reader; Chaucer's contemporaries, however, were so steeped in the theories of symbolism that it must have been difficult for them not to ask what every literary character and event represented. No passage or character of the Bible had escaped the efforts of scholars to discover signs and symbols and layers of meaning. This habit of thought spilled over into the reading of every kind of literature. Chaucer's audience would expect to find him providing them not only with good stories and amusing characters, but also with food for deeper thought. Much of his irony springs from the contrast between reality and the commonly-understood 'ideals' to which the audience unthinkingly subscribed.

Into the category of smaller and finer ironies we might put the verbal ironies, the playing on words, in which medieval audiences delighted. Only when the meaning of a word is well and commonly understood is it possible for a writer to make puns on its meaning. Chaucer's modern readers are at a serious disadvantage because it is extremely difficult to be sure that we have perceived the shades of meaning attached to a word which has changed or lost its meaning since; terms such as *'gentillesse'* and *'courtesie'* are obvious examples here. Similarly, it is very difficult for us to understand what Chaucer intended by ironies of manner. The reader of a story can put inflections into his voice which make it perfectly clear to his listeners that he is teasing, or that he means what he says half-humorously, or that he is apologising for what comes next. The written word cannot convey these nuances, although we can catch some glimpses of Chaucer's ironies of manner in his descriptions of the bearing and gestures of some of the pilgrims.

What have been called 'structural ironies' are also partly lost to us; within the 'Marriage Group' of tales Chaucer provides us with contrasts and striking juxtapositions which give added spice to the telling of the tales; but for a considerable part of the *Tales* we cannot be sure of the order or of the pattern which Chaucer intended his tales to form, because he never brought them into their final shape. Here, too, we can only glimpse Chaucer's irony. The dramatic side of Chaucer's irony is revealed only in certain of the tales, where pace and dialogue operate almost as they would do in the theatre to bewilder the reader.

Since so much of Chaucer's intended irony is hidden from us, the presence of so much that is recognizable and striking is a testimony to his immense skill as an ironist.

[1] W. Caxton Proem to *Canterbury Tales*, 1484 [2] Sir P. Sidney *Apology for Poetry*, 1595 [3] J. Dryden Preface to *Fables Ancient and Modern*, 1700 [4] G. Hazlitt *On Chaucer and Spencer: Lectures on English Poets*, *II*, 1818 [5] E. T. Donaldson *Chaucer's Poetry: An Anthology for the Modern Reader* (Ronald, 1958)

9

Chaucer's Audience

Chaucer wrote works which he intended his listeners to hear read aloud, rather than to read for themselves. Whatever the poet's original intentions, most readers of poetry today probably meet poems most often on the printed page. Chaucer was heir to a long tradition of poetry readings after dinner, which were probably closer to modern television programmes in their general appeal than to the formal poetry-readings which sometimes take place today— or even poetry and jazz sessions. Chaucer's audience listened to poetry-readings simply because they found them entertaining; they were not serious students of great literature, but ordinary people who enjoyed a good story.

35. This well-known picture of Chaucer reading his poem to the court comes from the Corpus Christi College, Cambridge manuscript of *Troilus and Criseyde*. On the face of it, it would suggest that the readings took place before a sizeable audience, and that the reader was given a place of honour—or at least eminence— while he spoke. Chaucer appears to be regarded as an honoured after-dinner speaker rather than a hired professional entertainer. But the picture was painted many years after the event, and may amount to no more than a conventional portrayal. (CCCC MS. 61)

The *Iliad* and the *Odyssey* of Homer, *The Epic of Beowulf* in Anglo-Saxon England, formed part of just such a long tradition of poetry written to be read or sung aloud; probably the tale was told in instalments, like a serial. These long stories in verse must have had something of the appeal of a modern novel, or a television serial, with one important exception. The modern reader expects a novel to have an unfamiliar plot; a great deal of his pleasure and interest comes from the desire to find out how the story ends. Detective stories, in particular, rely on the unexpected dénouement to keep their readers' attention to the end. Most of Chaucer's stories were borrowed or adapted from existing stories; in a similar way, the *Iliad* and the *Odyssey* dealt with well-known legends and characters whose fates the audiences would have known beforehand. The audience's interest had, therefore, to be captured and held by the actual telling of the tale. Thus the use of digressions, illustrations and 'asides' are all means of enlivening the tale. Chaucer flatters, indulges, dominates his audience, or addresses them confidentially, letting them in on secrets known only to the poet.

The audience and the readership for such poems were members of the aristocratic and administrative classes—the class to which Chaucer himself belonged. There were professional minstrels or 'singers of tales': the *troubadours* of 12th-century France who told the epic poems, or set the lyrics to music. But Chaucer did not make his living from poetry. It may not even have been Chaucer who read his poems aloud. In a sense he was an amateur poet, the equivalent of the 'Sunday painter' of today, because he was not dependent for his livelihood on the patronage of the arts which was financed by the upper classes.

Members of those wealthy and substantial families for which Chaucer wrote liked to possess books if they could afford them. The cost of producing a fine manuscript was of course enormous, so such possessions cannot have been common, and they must have been a source of immense pride to their owners. It was common in the later Middle Ages for bookshops to produce volumes in parts, called 'fascicles'. In this way a family could gradually build up its collection into a handsome volume.

In the mid-13th century, poems such as the stories in verse of *King Horn*, or *Floris and Blauncheflor* seem to have been popular reading. Certain elaborately-written and illuminated manuscripts are known to have been possessed by specific families. The *Très Riches Heures* of the Duc de Berry is a well-known continental example of a beautiful volume of religious texts owned and commissioned by a layman. In England there were commercial book-shops which copied such manuscripts and decorated them. The Auchinleck Manuscript, written about 1340, contains more than a dozen romances and a number of religious pieces. The Thornton Manuscript, packed with romances, came into the possession of Robert Thornton, lord of the manor of East Newton, Yorkshire, a century later. Perhaps the educated children of such substantial landowners used to read aloud to their parents in the evenings, in much the same way as a Victorian young lady was expected to be able to play and sing for the entertainment of her parents' guests.

The existence of a reading public was a comparative novelty. The wealthy middle classes came to expect higher standards of luxury in the appointments and fittings of their homes; domestic architecture developed to fulfil their demands. Houses were built of more durable materials, of brick and stone, with private rooms in which members of the family might spend their leisure in reading. Earlier dwellings had consisted chiefly of one large common room, which must have been noisy, dark, cluttered, and quite unsuitable for

36. A margin illustration depicting a game of chess, from the *Romance of Alexander*, written in Flanders *c.* 1340 (Bodleian MS. Bodl. 264 f. 112)

uninterrupted enjoyment of an elaborately produced book. The scriveners, or bookshops, which copied the books, supplied a demand for luxurious and rich decoration, great size and fine bindings. As a result, the books must often have been almost too heavy to lift and certainly too cumbersome to read comfortably, except at a bookstand of the kind we find in contemporary illustrations, but such elegant volumes were perhaps seen by their owners as signs of wealth and as valuable properties, as well as books to be read.

37. A bookstand. (Bodleian MS. Rawl. G 185 f. 81)

Easier and more frequent contacts with Europe must, too, have made more members of the merchant classes aware of the value and pleasure of books. Volumes produced in Europe include some particularly fine examples. The expanding universities, too, created a demand for books, often of course much plainer texts, for the use of students, who could afford only to hire them in sections, a few pages at a time. But the bookshops which copied the texts had a place in the growing industry of secular book production.

There was no rigid class-distinction in England between the members of the aristocracy proper and those families which engaged in trade and provided recruits for the civil service and the administration. The situation was very different on the Continent, but we know that Chaucer's family of well-to-do vintners was able to send him to court to begin his career. Thus Chaucer's audience was not restricted solely to the aristocracy whose profession and whose pastime was still the bearing of arms. Courtly poetry in France had been almost exclusively the poetry of romance and chivalry, and, while such verses had a strong appeal in England, and closely influenced Chaucer himself, he could write about the members of a wide range of social classes and of a number of 'degrees' and still captivate his audience:

> *To telle yow al the condicioun*
> *Of ech of hem, so as it semed me,*
> *And whiche they weren, and of what degree.*

Chaucer ran no risk of boring his audience with the altogether unfamiliar, nor of offending aristocratic sensibilities in writing about the members of the lower social classes.

IO

Editing Chaucer

A modern novel comes to its reader neatly packaged in a single volume. If it becomes a bestseller, it will be reprinted and even if alterations are made in later editions, the work as a whole remains substantially the same. The author's original drafts, his early revisions of the text, his false starts and second thoughts, are not as a rule counted as a part of the text of the finished novel. But in the case of Chaucer's *Canterbury Tales*, it is precisely these experimental drafts and first or second attempts which have come down to us. *The Canterbury Tales* was never published in a final form, because it was never finished.

Even if Chaucer had polished it and shaped it to his own final satisfaction before it left his hands, it would have differed from a modern novel in an important respect: no publisher's editor would have worked over it, suggesting improvements and pruning it with commercially expert fingers. Chaucer's versions of his *Tales* are his own compositions, and they do not bear the marks of another mind.

Chaucer's works, like those of every other medieval author, were written in manuscript. This means that every book which was written before the invention of printing (which took place nearly a hundred years after Chaucer's death) has had to be rendered into print by a process of meticulous editing. In some cases, only a single manuscript of a work survives, and there is no way of knowing how close this version comes to the work as it was originally written by its author. A great many short poems of Chaucer's day come into this category. If there is more than one surviving manuscript, a whole range of new problems presents itself. Could any one of the manuscripts have been written by the author himself, or are they all copies made by others? There are no 'autograph' manuscripts (that is, manuscripts in Chaucer's own hand) to help settle disputes over the texts of his poems. Is manuscript C a copy of manuscript B, and is B a copy of A, with a consequent multiplication of mistakes in each successive copy? Or are manuscripts A and B both copies of C, which agree with it in certain details, but perhaps have variations of their own as a result of their own copyists' errors? Are A and B copies of a lost manuscript C? Is there a group of manuscripts which are all copies of A and another group of copies of B? Even if a 'family tree' of manuscripts can be worked out by a careful comparison of differences, the editor's task is not over.

He has to decide which of his manuscripts represents the best version of the work, and to do that he must know his author's habits of thought and style very well. When he has decided on the methods and principles of selection which he will use in establishing his text, he still has to contend with the problems raised by difficult-to-read handwriting, mistakes made in copying, accidental loss of a few leaves of the manuscript, or damage to the pages. Damp or worm-holes may leave gaps in the text. Sheer hard wear by readers of a popular part of the text may have rubbed out the words. Occasionally, part of a manuscript may have been used as scrap paper to bind other books, in a later century; it is not unknown for fragments of older texts to be found inside bindings.

A further set of minute difficulties meets the editor, even when he has decided upon the best source to follow in establishing his text, and upon his principles of editing. He has to expand the abbreviations with which all medieval scribes shortened their task of copying, and he has to do it in such a way that his spelling of the words Chaucer used represents Chaucer's own practice. Since there is no surviving manuscript which was written by Chaucer himself, he has no standard of comparison. Grammatical accuracy must be preserved as well as the essentially Chaucerian flavour of the style.

In *The Knight's Tale*, for example, a large number of manuscripts read: '*And he hire serveth so gentilly*', while the Harleian manuscript reads: '*And he hire serveth also gentilly*', which seems to preserve a better rhythm. Is the editor to prefer: '*For to have been a marchal in an halle*' or: '*For to been a marchal in an halle*'? (*Gen Prol.* 1.752), when the manuscripts offer him alternative readings?

Chaucer's poetry never entirely lost its popularity, and numerous copies were made. The editor's job is therefore immensely complicated. About ninety manuscripts and early printed versions of *The Canterbury Tales*, some complete as far as we have the *Tales*, some fragmentary, have had to be taken into account. Eight manuscripts have been published by the Chaucer Society, and they include some of the best authorities. The Ellesmere manuscript is probably the best-known, because of its amusing and frequently reproduced illustrations of the pilgrims. This manuscript belongs to a group which has been classified as the 'A' type of manuscript. A second group, which seems to represent a less sound tradition, has been called 'B'. But despite its general inferiority, the 'B' group sometimes provides a better reading of specific words or phrases. One manuscript, the Harleian manuscript, is particularly puzzling. It

38. A page of the Harleian manuscript. (BM MS. Harley 7334)

appears to belong in the main to group 'B', but it contains several readings which belong to type 'A'. Some of its versions are unique. Early editors, in particular Skeat, suggested that this manuscript might contain copies of some of Chaucer's own revisions. (Although he never finished the *Tales* as a whole, there is every reason to think that Chaucer polished and revised some parts of what he had already written.) But it seems more probable that the manuscript contains yet another kind of trap for the editor: a scribe might make alterations of his own in copying a manuscript if he could not understand the copy he had before him, or even because he thought he could improve upon it.

In the case of *Troilus and Criseyde*, the manuscripts seem to suggest that Chaucer composed the poem in at least two stages, and possibly in three. The first version has been called α and it is very much closer to the Italian version from which Chaucer drew in writing the poem, than is version γ. A 'middle version' has been called β. If these three versions really represent three separate stages of composition, the editor has a quite different problem from that which faces the editor of *The Canterbury Tales*; he has to decide which of these three versions represents the 'real' *Troilus*; he has to choose between them. Alternatively, Chaucer may have left unfinished versions in which there is no sequence of revision, but only stray pieces of rethinking.

The Book of the Duchess and *The House of Fame* present yet a third editorial problem. They survive in only a few manuscripts which agree with each other quite well. But their similarities do not necessarily mean that they represent the 'right' text. They merely represent the text we happen to have.

Chaucer's editors have been numerous. Skeat, the great Victorian scholar who laid the foundations of modern scholarship in Old and Middle English, produced the first modern edition in 1894–7. Manly's edition of 1928 comprised only *The Canterbury Tales*. More recently, F. N. Robinson has established what is still, for most scholars, the definitive edition of Chaucer's entire known works. The text of Manly and Rickert (Chicago, 1940) has not in general been thought better. The Chaucerian scholars of today still rely to a considerable extent upon the Robinson version.

THE ARRANGEMENT OF THE TALES

Chaucer probably decided to write the *Tales* in about 1386. It seems that he wrote the *General Prologue* in 1387, and for several years he appears to have been working on the *Tales*, some of which were almost certainly written as late as 1393–4. He may even have gone on working on them for the rest of his life, perhaps in patches as fresh ideas came to him, or as leisure allowed him to take up the work and revise what he had written. Chaucer had planned for each of the pilgrims to tell two tales on the journey to Canterbury, and two tales on the way home, if the *General Prologue* is to be taken at its word. As it stands, the *Tales* includes only twenty-three stories, of which some remain unfinished; others appear not to belong to their tellers. (The Shipman, for instance, once or twice calls himself a woman.) Obviously, Chaucer never got as far as revising his stories in readiness to have them published as a whole, nor did he assemble even the ones he had finished in their final order.

We cannot be sure what that order was to be. The tales which survive are arranged in some of the apparently most reliable manuscripts in an order which cannot possibly be the one Chaucer would finally have intended. Tales which were told as the pilgrims neared Canterbury come before tales which were told soon after they set out, to judge from the geographical signposts which Chaucer occasionally provides. The tales come down to us in fragments which are conventionally labelled, A, B, C, D, E, F, G, H, I.

The first fragment, A, contains the *General Prologue*, *The Knight's Tale*, *The Miller's Tale* and those of the Reeve and the Cook. *The Knight's Tale* is a chivalric romance which contrasts strongly with the scurrilous and disreputable stories which follow it. *The Cook's Tale* is unfinished and the fragment ends there. The second fragment, B¹, begins with *The Man of Law's Tale*. It is impossible to be sure that this is meant to come next. The Cook's unfinished tale provides no link with what is to follow. The Man of Law's *Prologue* compounds the problem. He says that he will speak in prose, but his tale is told in verse. This fragment, then, occupies an uncertain position. The third fragment in the best manuscripts is D. This contains the first of seven stories on aspects of marriage, which is sometimes called the 'Marriage Debate or Group'. These stories seem, by their continuity, to have been carefully welded together by Chaucer. In the 'Marriage Group' fall the tales of the Wife of Bath, the Friar, the Summoner, in group E (fragment four) *The Clerk's Tale*, followed by the tale of the Merchant with *The Squire's Tale* and *The Franklin's Tale* in F (fragment five).

The sixth fragment (C) breaks the continuity again. *The Physician's Tale* and *The Pardoner's Tale* stand apart. The seventh fragment (B²) contains *The Shipman's Tale*, *The Prioress's Tale*,

Chaucer's own two stories, (the abortive *Sir Topas*, which the Host interrupts, and *The Tale of Melibee*), together with *The Monk's Tale* and *The Nun's Priest's Tale*.

Again there is a break in continuity. The eighth fragment, G, has *The Second Nun's Tale*, and that of *The Canon's Yeoman*. *The Manciple's Tale* begins fragment nine, H, where the pilgrims are at Bob-up-and-down, probably very close to Canterbury. It is possible that this tale was intended for the journey back. The final fragment contains *The Parson's Tale* (I) which, it has been suggested, was perhaps to be saved for the very end of the journey.

Whatever solutions may be proposed by Chaucer's editors to the problem of the proper arrangement of the tales, we shall never know for certain what the author's intentions were. As he left the work, it is impossible to be sure of more than a few of the links between tales. But Chaucer was not concerned that the details of the progress of the pilgrimage should tally exactly with the length of the tales; his interest lay in the exchanges between the pilgrims and in the telling of the tales themselves. His literary training had taught him a different kind of exactness from that with which we are familiar.

11

Chaucer and His Influence

Chaucer was an important figure in the eyes of the poets of the 15th century. A number of poets in Scotland as well as in England have traditionally been called 'Chaucerians' because they were thought to have admired and imitated him as a master, or at least followed in his footsteps. Some of these poets might be surprised, and none too pleased, at the label which has been attached to them. Just as the term 'Romantic Poets' is used to describe collectively the strongly contrasted Blake, Wordsworth, Coleridge, Keats, Shelley, Byron; so the 'Chaucerians' include a widely assorted variety of individual poets.

It is important to remember that Chaucer did not invent English poetry. In the north of England in the 14th century alliterative verse was still flourishing in the Old English tradition to which *Beowulf* belongs, or perhaps it represents a reawakening of interest in that tradition. Such poetry pleased the ear by stringing together a succession of words with the same initial consonant; the effect was prevented from being too repetitive by the device of introducing a pause near the middle of the line very much like the *cesura* of Classical Latin verse, where a natural pause interrupts the flow of the line. The effect is to give the ear a rest from an otherwise monotonously insistent rhythm or metre.

A witty, sophisticated 'scholar's poetry' flourished among the clergy. It had a good deal in common with its Latin counterparts, those polished and neatly-turned lyrics, and narratives which scholars enjoyed:

De ramis cadunt folia
  nam viror totus periit
Nam calor liquit omnia
  et abiit;
Nam signa coeli ultima
  sol petiit.[1]

Down from the branches fall the leaves
A wanness comes on all the trees,

> *The summer's done,*
> *And into his last house in heaven*
> *Now goes the sun.*

The Owl and the Nightingale is a poem of this kind written in English, some time after 1200. Its subject-matter consists of a debate between two birds who represent, respectively, the serious student who cannot be persuaded to abandon his books and enjoy himself, and the work-shy student who is far more interested in having a good time than in getting his degree.

A third type of poetry had a stronger appeal to the middle-class society to which Chaucer belonged: *King Horn, The Lay of Havelok the Dane, Floris and Blauncheflor* were stories in verse of the middle of the 13th century. They were packed with dialogue and events, and without the long passages of description and the references to classical heroes which were to be found in the high romances. All serious scholarship was carried out in Latin; these stories seemed by contrast intellectually undemanding, easy to read or to listen to. They may be compared with ballad-stories such as 'John Gilpin' in their simple appeal as good stories.

Chaucer, then, was heir to several poetic traditions, which he was in an unusually good position to straddle. We know that his education and his travelling had fitted him to translate from Latin, and to read French and probably Italian. He could approach the scholars on their own ground; on the other hand, he was not a professional scholar, or a member of the clergy, and so he remained closely in touch with the tastes and interests of his own middle-class friends in the civil service and with the perhaps more aristocratic tastes of the court. His achievement was to fashion out of what had gone before a kind of poetry which drew on elements of all that he knew; from the Classical references to Caesar and Pompey, to Apollo, to Virgil, Ovid and Homer, in *The House of Fame*, to the sharply personal observation of the behaviour of ordinary people which gives *The Canterbury Tales* their universal and lasting appeal. D. S. Brewer talks of 'two cultures' in Chaucer's day, by which he means not C. P. Snow's 'two cultures' of the 20th century, the scientific and artistic, but the Latin and vernacular cultures of the Middle Ages. Chaucer had some command of both.

Chaucer's successors, like Chaucer himself, inherited the skills and poetic tradition which were the result of a long process of development. They seem to have admired Chaucer's *Parliament of Fowls, Troilus and Criseyde,* and *The Legend of Good Women* because they are examples of familiar types of composition. John Lydgate (1370–1449) for example, wrote a great deal, taking laborious care in composition. His poem about Henry VI's triumphal entry into London was written, as were others among his works, to celebrate

39. These glass-blowers are the subject of one of the twenty-eight miniatures which illustrate the first five chapters of *The Travels of Sir John Mandeville* in a 15th century manuscript. (BM MS. 5 Add. 24189 f. 16)

40. Here the artist has represented Lydgate as a pilgrim; he has all the traditional accoutrements: staff, hat, wallet with scallop shell, rough woollen garment. He is presenting his poem, *The Pilgrim*, to his patron, Thomas Montacute, Earl of Salisbury, whose knighthood is signified by the armour he wears. Despite the stylized conventionality of the poses and the idealization of the scene, the portrayal of the faces of Lydgate and the Earl of Salisbury suggests that the artist had some skill in conveying expression. The picture cannot with certainty be called a portrait of Lydgate, although it has some claims to be so. Medieval artists obeyed a whole set of conventions of representation which made it much more important to show details of dress and position, than to attempt to paint an accurate picture of their subjects' faces—even if they were in a position to do so. (BM MS. 13 Harley 4826 f. 1*)

a special occasion. He embarked with earnest industriousness upon a 25,000-line translation of the *Pilgrimage of the Life of Man* by Deguileville which was commissioned by the Earl of Salisbury, and he wrote a 30,000-line *Troy Book* on the story of the fall of Troy, again on commission, this time from Prince Henry. He seems to have attempted to organize Chaucer's fresh and often icono-clastic ideas into formal techniques. As Derek Pearsall remarks: '*One fault of his versification is not that it is irregular, but that it is too systematically, ruthlessly, monotonously regular.*'[2] Lydgate may perhaps be viewed as primarily a craftsman rather than an artist.

There can be no doubt of his admiration for Chaucer's achieve-ment. Compliments were paid to Chaucer's skills as a poet by more than one of the 'Chaucerians'; such remarks have a certain con-ventionality but are none the less sincere. Lydgate praises him for having refashioned the English language as a vehicle for poetry, for having given it the flexibility and fine-tuned precision to express the whole range of rhetorical skills:

> *My mayster Chaunceer did his besynesse*
> *And in his dayes hath so wel hym born*
> *Out of our tounge tauoyden al Rudnesse*
> *And to Reffourme it with Colours of swetnesse.*[3]

Thomas Hoccleve was a personal acquaintance of Chaucer's, a clerk in the office of the Privy Seal, who died about 1430, and was probably more than twenty years Chaucer's junior. His verse has a pleasant irony, and he is able, like Chaucer, to laugh at himself. But in contrast to Lydgate, he does not seem to have made laborious efforts to imitate Chaucer. His writing is clear and simple, regular in rhythm, without fancy adornments, workmanlike and unaffected. His longest poem, *The Regement of Princes* (1412) is a handbook of moral instruction for princes. In the dialogue with which the poem begins, Hoccleve complains to a beggar about his worries, the difficulties of keeping out of debt, the effects of being middle-aged—subject-matter which, if it is not entirely new, is at any rate strikingly down-to-earth in contrast with the pretensions implied in the title of the poem. His lament for Chaucer and Gower rails at Death for slaying these two great poets:

> *O maister deere, and fader reverent!*
> *My maister Chaucer, flowr of eloquence,*
> *Mirour of fructuous entendement,*
> *O universal fader in science!*

Allas that thou thyn excellent prudence
In thy bed mortal mightest nought bequethe
What ailed deth? Allas! Why would he slee thee?[4]

The Kingis Quair is a 'love-vision' poem, of a kind familiar
in Chaucer's works and in the literature of his day in general. Only
one manuscript of this work is known, and it names James I of
Scotland as the author. The poem is written in a literary southern
English, with some Scottish overtones, and it bears some marks
of the Chaucer tradition. But it is an eclectic poem, where a number
of traditions make their influence felt. Even in his use of poetic
devices, the poet shows himself a willing borrower. There are
passages of description, of song, of prayer, of moralizing, of dialogue, of complaint, of dream or vision. The poet begins by telling
how, during a sleepless night, he read that standby and inspiration
of all kinds of medieval writers—Boethius' *Consolation of Philosophy*. The poem is perhaps of interest precisely because it includes
examples of so many contemporary poetical practices; it is very
much the product of its age:

The lyoun king, and his fere lyonesse;
The pantere, like unto the smaragdyne;
The lytill squerell, ful of besynesse,
The slaw ase, the druggar, beste of pyne;
The nyce ape; the werely porpapyne;
The percyng lynx; the lufare unicorne
That voidis venym with his evour horne.

There saw I dress him new out of haunt
The fery tiger, full of felonye;
The dromydare; the standar oliphant;
The wyly fox, the wedowys inemye;
The clymbare gayte; the elk for alblastrye;
The herknere bore; the holsum grey for hortis;
The haie also, that oft gooth to the wortis.[5]

In these stanzas the author describes a series of beasts in a list
which is of a common and conventional kind, but the beasts have
a certain liveliness and charm which raises the descriptions above
the commonplace.

During the 15th and early part of the 16th centuries Scottish
poetry flourished. The most important poets, or 'makaris', of this
time, Henryson, Dunbar and Douglas, have been called the Scottish

Chaucerians, a somewhat misleading title. Their language, Middle Scots, was a variant of northern English and a literary language in its own right. But they did admire and were influenced by Chaucer, whom Dunbar called the '*rose of rethoris all*', the flower of the schools of rhetoric. To Douglas, he seems the finest of poets, and thus worthy of reverence and emulation:

> . . . *Venerabill Chauser, principal poet but peir,*
> *Hevynly trumpat, orlege and reguler,*
> *In eloquens balmy cundyt and dyall,*
> *Mylky fontane, cleir strand and roys ryall*
> *Of fresch endyte, throu Albion iland braid.*[6]

But these poets may have had no very clear notion of the nature of Chaucer's achievement. Some of Lydgate's poems had been ascribed to Chaucer, and it is possible that what they admired was the work of the greatest English poets as a whole; Chaucer, Gower and Lydgate may all have been regarded, almost collectively, as examples of excellence.

Robert Henryson was a Dunfermline schoolmaster who died about 1500; William Dunbar was a Master of Arts of the University of St. Andrews, who was given a pension by James IV of Scotland. His poems were mostly composed between 1500 and 1513. Gavin Douglas was a younger son of the fifth Earl of Angus born about 1475; he, too, graduated from the University of St. Andrews, and rapidly made his mark in the Church. Like Chaucer, all these poets had professions which made them independent of poetry as a means of earning a living. Like Chaucer, they wrote in a wide variety of *genres* of poetry. William Dunbar, in particular, was capable of writing anything, from the bawdiest of verse to elaborate, dignified, formally elegant poems of praise to the great or the holy. His hymn to the Virgin Mary, 'Ane Ballat of Our Lady', shows how gracefully he could turn a verse:

> *Empryce of prys, imperatrice*
> *Brycht polist precious stane,*
> *Victrice of vyce, hie genetrice,*
> *Of Jhesu, lord soverayne.*[7]

The internal rhymes (which are a feature of the Latin hymns Dunbar was probably imitating here) make this technically a very difficult form to use. The scholar is evident in the 'Lament for the Makaris', where each stanza ends with a Latin tag: 'The fear of death horrifies me.'

> *I that in heill wes and gladnes,*
> *Am trublit now with gret seiknes,*
> *And feblit with infermite;*
> Timor mortis conturbat me.

> *Our plesance heir is all vane glory,*
> *This fals warld is bot transitory,*
> *The flesche is brukle, the Fend is sle;*
> Timor mortis conturbat me.[8]

Dunbar is saying nothing new; innumerable medieval writers had expressed similar sentiments on the subject of the transitoriness of the good things of this world, and the need for the Christian to remember that he must die and face judgment. But the conventional ideas are neatly expressed, and the Latin tag falls into place with that apparent inevitability which is a sure sign of mastery of technique, if not of great art.

Henryson's *The Testament of Cresseid* demands comparison with *Troilus and Criseyde*; the poet describes how he sits down to write, in winter, and thinks about Chaucer's poem. He adds a postscript to it, in the form of an account of how Troilus meets Cresseid, stricken with leprosy, fails to recognize her, and gives her alms. Cresseid speaks to the members of her own sex, the fair ladies of Troy and of Greece, warning them that their beauty will fade, and that Fortune is fickle:

> *Nocht is your fairnes bot ane faiding flour,*
> *Nocht is your famous laud and hie honour*
> *Bot wind Inflat in uther mennis eiris . . .*
> *Fortoun is fikkill . . . .*[9]

Again, the thought is commonplace; these academic poets were familiar with a set of conventions which governed not only style and form, but also the appropriate views to be expressed on any one of a given range of topics. But the technical skill eases the thought gracefully into place. Henryson was so much a master of technique that his poetry often appears simpler than it is. Their technical competence, and their ability to use it in writing a variety of different kinds of poem, makes these craftsmanlike Scottish poets more than pale imitators of Chaucer's achievement. Henryson, for example, rarely uses the Chaucerian couplet, but prefers to write in stanzas. He has little taste for Chaucer's humour. Douglas probably modelled his *Palace of Honour* on Chaucer's *The House of Fame* but added touches of his own.

The Scottish Chaucerians were admirers of Chaucer, but not close imitators. They borrowed ideas, devices, whatever was relevant to their needs. But the title which they have been traditionally given is an artificial one; like most attempts to label a group of individuals a 'school' of poets or artists, it imposes an apparent uniformity on a variety of different achievements. What is perhaps most significant is the fact that it is Chaucer's name which has been imposed upon them. Their title is, more than anything else, a tribute to Chaucer's lasting reputation.

[1] F. J. E. Raby (Ed.) *The Oxford Book of Medieval Latin Verse* (O.U.P., 1959) p. 353   [2] D. Pearsall in *Chaucer and the Chaucerians* ed. D. S. Brewer (Nelson, 1970) p. 206   [3] C. F. E. Spurgeon *Five Hundred Years of Chaucer Criticism and Allusion, I* (C.U.P., 1925) p. 37   [4] Sisam and Sisam (Eds.) *The Oxford Book of Medieval English Verse* (O.U.P., 1970) p. 379   [5] J. Norton-Smith (Ed.) *Kingis Quair* (O.U.P., 1971) p. 39   [6] Gavin Douglas *Aeneid* Book I   [7] D. S. Brewer (Ed.) *Chaucer and the Chaucerians* (Nelson, 1970) p. 181   [8] W. M. Mackenzie (Ed.) *The Poems of William Dunbar* (Faber, 1932)   [9] H. H. Wood *The Poems and Fables of Robert Henryson* (Oliver & Boyd, 1958) p. 121.

12

The Chaucer Industry

Geoffrey Chaucer's poetry has never gone completely out of favour. Both critics and the ordinary reader have found something to enjoy in him in every age. But his appeal has not always been the same. The reader finds in Chaucer what he is looking for, and what he expects to find is to some extent decided by the tastes of his day. In the late 15th and early 16th centuries Chaucer's poetry was sometimes considered rustic and simple, written in archaic language, but his humour gave pleasure even to the 16th century purists who wanted to make the English language a more finely-tuned instrument of expression. George Puttenham wrote in the *Art of English Poesy* (1589): '*In the Canterbury Tales Chaucer showeth more the natural of his pleasant wit than in any other of his works.*'

Even the 19th century reader who felt that Shakespeare and Milton wrote works of greater stature, moment and dignity, appreciated his presentation of what they regarded as a middle-class very much like that of their own day. Chaucer's poetry appeared in very different lights to the critics of different ages. It is a measure of its greatness that so many people have found in it what they looked for. The Chaucer bibliographies grow fuller every year.

Chaucer's earliest critics admired him for the quality of his poetry and his use of language above all else. Quite understandably, the more remote in time his writing became, the more other aspects of his work came into prominence, and his language came to be seen almost as a barrier to a proper contact with his work. So began the paraphrasing and translation of Chaucer which has gone on ever since.

Chaucer was particularly well served by some of the earliest critics who turned their hands to this task because they were considerable poets themselves. Amongst the earliest and most distinguished of them was John Dryden whose *Fables, Ancient and Modern* (1700) contained versions of three of the Canterbury tales (*The Knight's*; *The Nun's Priest's*; and *The Wife of Bath's*) together with 'The Character of a Good Parson'. The 'Preface' to the

Fables remains a distinguished piece of Chaucerian criticism. One of Dryden's distinctive qualities was that he was one of the earliest critics actually to criticize Chaucer's work. He praises him highly:

> *He is the father of English poetry, so I hold him in the same degree of veneration as the Grecians held Homer, or the Romans Virgil. He is a perpetual fountain of good sense; learned in all sciences; and, therefore, speaks properly on all subjects ....*
> *Chaucer followed Nature everywhere, but was never so bold to go beyond her.*

but he adds: '*The verse of Chaucer, I confess, is not harmonious to us .... We can only say, that he lived in the infancy of our poetry, and that nothing is brought to perfection at first.*'

Dryden lived in the age of 'good sense' when there was a great emphasis placed upon the notions of decorum and correctness in verse. Therefore he has reservations about '*the ribaldry, which is very gross*' of some of the tales, and in his translation attempts to adapt Chaucer to the tastes of his time:

> *I have not tied myself to a literal translation; but have omitted what I judged unnecessary, or not of dignity enough to appear in the company of better thoughts. I have presumed further in some places, and added somewhat of my own where I thought my author was deficient, and had not given his thoughts their true lustre, for want of words in the beginning of our language ....*

41. William Blake   *The Canterbury Pilgrims*   (British Museum)

Another poet, in another age, may take the same liberty with my writings; if at least they live long enough to deserve correction.

However, in spite of his reservations, Dryden recognizes that in Chaucer '*Here is God's plenty*' and his own version of 'the fables' is a distinguished piece of writing by any standards, only exceeded as a translation by Pope's version of *The Wife of Bath's Tale* in 1714. The Chaucer industry was by now well under way.

The next major writer to find inspiration in Chaucer was William Blake, who in 1809 published his *Descriptive Catalogue*, to accompany his painting, *The Canterbury Pilgrims*, now in the British Museum. Thus Blake relates his work to Chaucer's:

The characters of Chaucer's Pilgrims are the characters which compose all ages and nations . . . some of the names or titles are altered by time, but the characters themselves forever remain unaltered . . . . As Newton numbered the stars . . . so Chaucer numbered the classes of men.

The Painter has consequently varied the heads and forms of his personages into all Nature's varieties; the Horses he has also varied to accord to their Riders; the costume is correct according to authentic monuments.

Blake continues to describe the whole company of Pilgrims. For example, of the Host he writes:

URY PILGRIMS

[the Host] *who holds the centre of the cavalcade, is a first rate character, and his jokes are no trifles; they are always, though uttered with audacity, and equally free with the Lord and Peasant, they are always substantially and weightily expressive of knowledge and experience; Henry Baillie, the keeper of the greatest Inn of the greatest City; for such was the Tabarde Inn in Southwark, our Host was also a leader of the age.*

The last of the great 19th century critics of Chaucer was Matthew Arnold, who in his *Essays in Criticism* (1865 and 1888) recognized the genius of the poet and also located that genius in the quality of the language that he wrote. He saw Chaucer as being superior to other writers of his time, many of whom, like him, fascinated their contemporaries:

Chaucer's power of fascination, however, is enduring . . . . He is a genuine source of joy and strength, which is flowing still for us and will flow always. He will be read, as time goes on, far more generally than he is read now. His language is a cause of difficulty for us; but so also, and I think in quite as great a degree, is the language of Burns. In Chaucer's case, as in that of Burns, it is a difficulty to be unhesitatingly accepted and overcome.

Arnold saw the superiority of Chaucer as lying in the superiority of his subject matter and in his style. He quotes with approval Dryden's earlier comment: '*Here is God's plenty,*' and he points to the '*perpetual fountain of good sense*' that Chaucer represents. But it is above all the '*fluid movement*' of the verse that is the source of his strength, Chaucer's greatness is *because of*, not as some earlier critics had suggested, *in spite of* his language:

A nation may have versifiers with smooth numbers and easy rhymes, and yet may have no real poetry at all. Chaucer is the father of our splendid English poetry . . . by the lovely charm of his diction, the lovely charm of his movement, he makes an epoch and founds a tradition.

In a very telling passage Arnold compares an extract from Chaucer's *Prioress's Tale* with a 19th century version by Wordsworth in which, as he convincingly shows, '*the charm is departed*' —Chaucer remains superior as a writer to those who seek to interpret him in the form of modern paraphrase or translation.

It would be partial and unfair, however, to leave this brief account of Arnold's criticism of Chaucer without reference to what he saw as the poet's major failing; a failing he feels, which presents him from reaching classical stature:

> *To our praise of Chaucer as a poet there must be this limitation; he lacks the high seriousness of the great classics, and therewith an important part of their virtue. Still, the main fact for us to bear in mind about Chaucer is his sterling value according to that real estimate which we firmly adopt for all poets. He has poetic truth of substance, though he has not high poetic seriousness, and corresponding to his truth of substance he has an exquisite virtue of style and manner. With him is born our real poetry.*

This is high praise indeed and we may feel that the moral earnestness of the late Victorians that rings through the demand for the quality of '*high seriousness*' tells us more about Arnold than it does about Chaucer. But the admiration, the enjoyment, the love of Chaucer is certainly there and the discovery of this enjoyment in the quality of the language and the rhythm of the verse demonstrates a characteristic sensitivity in Arnold's response.

Along with this kind of informed criticism the 19th century saw the beginning of modern Chaucerian scholarship. In 1868, Furnival founded the Chaucer Society which published a number of Chaucer materials, including some of the manuscripts, and the foundations for modern linguistic scholarship in Middle English were laid by the monumental seven-volume Chaucer published in 1894–7.

The 20th century has seen the work of both scholarship and critical interpretation continuing; Chaucer is probably more widely read today than at any time previously. His language is no longer seen as setting up an impassable barrier and several of the tales are regularly set for school examinations, even at Ordinary level. J. A. Burrow's critical anthology on Geoffrey Chaucer is a useful collection of writings on the poet and forms a first-class introduction to modern scholarship.

Along with the work of interpretation has gone an extensive movement towards the popularization of Chaucer. The leading name in this field has been that of Nevill Coghill. In the late forties Coghill adapted a number of the tales, and produced verse paraphrases of them for reading on the radio. These readings were often accompanied by extracts from the same tales read in the original Middle English. These broadcasts and the records that developed from them made Chaucer accessible to a new and wider

K

public and it is striking that this expansion of interest in Chaucer through the 20th century medium of radio is directly equivalent to the oral tradition through which the text was transmitted in the first place. Some of the records are still available, and these will help to give the flavour of the radio broadcasts. In particular, readings by Coghill and others of *The General Prologue* and *The Nun's Priest's Tale* on the Argo label can be recommended for their sensitive treatment of Middle English verse and the skill in interpretation that is represented.

Unfortunately one cannot perhaps give the same unreserved praise to other aspects of the popularization of Chaucer with which Coghill has also been associated. In 1951 he produced a complete verse translation of *The Canterbury Tales*, which became an immediate bestseller. Even today many people know Chaucer primarily through Coghill's version and this may actually serve as a discouragement from going to the original and reading it for oneself. The very existence of a translation of this kind may help to promote the idea that there is something especially difficult, even foreign, about Chaucer's language, rather than that it is remarkably like the one that we speak today. The 19th century recognized the genius of that language and Arnold thought that Chaucer would be even more widely read in the future. It is to the shame of our present desire for instant results for the minimum expense of effort and engagement that Coghill has been substituted for Chaucer in the experience of many.

In his introduction to his version of *The Canterbury Tales*, Coghill makes clear what his motives are:

> *The present version of this masterwork is intended for those who feel difficulty in reading the original, yet would like to enjoy as much of that 'plenty' as the translator has been able to convey in a more modern idiom.*

There would be little point in criticizing Coghill's version if it were not in the form of verse, and if the author had not begun by quoting Dryden and Pope as his predecessors in the art of Chaucerian paraphrase. His quotation from Dryden's 'Preface' to the *Fables* is a telling one:

> *I have translated some parts of his works, only that I might perpetuate his memory, or at least refresh it, amongst my countrymen. If I have altered him anywhere for the better, I must at the same time acknowledge, that I could have done nothing without him . . . .*

Claiming this ancestry Coghill must expect to be judged by the highest standards.

Unhappily, for all his scholarship in the field, Professor Coghill's version seemed to many not to measure up to the test. A reviewer in *The Listener* when the book was first published touched off a vigorous controversy which related essentially to the literary value of Coghill's text. His comments were uncompromising:

> *This lamentable book is likely to be a gratuitous obstacle to a proper understanding of Chaucer. The ignorant reader will think (with the 'translator') that here is a satisfactory substitute for the true thing. Why, then, should he trouble to read the original? Indeed he has every excuse for refusing to do so. Let Mr Coghill speak for him: 'In the first place the pressure of contemporary life seems greatly to have increased upon us and many who would be willing to take pains to read him in the original are insufficiently at leisure to do so; secondly the original is not really so easy as all that'* .... *The fort is sold with a smile; and what a pleasant little bunch of excuses Mr. Coghill's own pupils* ... *have to their hand.*

The reviewer, using a technique that Arnold had applied to Wordsworth before him, points vividly to the vulgarization of Chaucer which this whole approach implies:

> *Chaucer's miraculous* fabliau *poems of the Miller and Reeve become in his hands merely a couple of bawdy stories* .... *The warm and vital Alisoun is reduced to a dull catalogue of attributes, without a blush for what is ruined. One of Chaucer's happiest touches is:*
> > *'She was ful moore blisful on to see*
> > *Than is the newe pereionette tree.'*
> *This dazzle of spring and grace of youth becomes the lumpish*
> > *'And a more truly blissful sight to see*
> > *She was than blossom on a cherry-tree.'*
> *The Host would have had a word for the worth of this 'drasty ryming.'*

The task is an impossible one for any except an extraordinarily gifted poet. An Alexander Pope can produce a verse translation of Chaucer because he is contributing something of his own genius as a poet to the work; but scholars are well advised to leave such things alone and stick to their own business. In any case Chaucer is not so very difficult to come to terms with in the original, especially if that original is read aloud, which is where Coghill's real contribution to making Chaucer available to a wider public lies. If we do need help in reading him we shall find that a straightforward prose paraphrase is the surest guide. David Wright's prose version of 1964 is to be especially recommended for its honesty to the original text, and Wright's own preface makes clear why his version is so much superior to other modern attempts at versifying:

> *I have thought it worthwhile to make the experiment of trans-lating* The Canterbury Tales *into straightforward contemporary prose . . . . The trouble with most verse translations . . . has been the pedestrian versification of the translators. One result has been not only to obscure the view of Chaucer's poetry, but too many of his other qualities, by the cataract of the makeshift and often downright bathetic rhyme-carpentry into which their efforts to reproduce the Tales in verse has led.*

Versions such as Wright's which have no literary pretension of their own are the surest way into Chaucer when help with the original is needed.

But the work of vulgarization has unfortunately not stopped there. In 1968 there appeared at the Phoenix Theatre in London a musical stage version of *The Canterbury Tales*, which was well summed up by the quotation from Harold Hobson's *Sunday Times* review which was used as bait to draw the crowds into the theatre for the five years during which the show ran: '*The raciest, bawdiest, most good hearted and good humoured show in London.*' According to Hobson the show had a '*farcical invention worthy of Feydeau and a daring far beyond him*'. It is no difficult matter to guess which of the *Tales* the show sought to dramatize and the further presentation of Chaucer as a minor talent with a fund of dirty stories was the main consequence of a show which nonetheless brought box-office success.

Finally we have had, almost inevitably, a film version of *The Canterbury Tales*, directed by Pasolini in 1973. Pasolini had earlier had something of a box office and artistic success with his film *The Decameron* and to turn to that from Chaucer was a natural step. However like most of those who have tried to make profit out of Chaucer without any real understanding of his greatness, Pasolini had taken on more than he was capable of handling and the film, for all the splendour of its costumes and settings, is an un-doubted failure and a further example of how in our century great art can be reduced to a mindless and tasteless mediocrity. Dilys

Powell in a contemporary review of the Pasolini film is worth attention:

> *What one rejects is not the foreign . . . but the boring. The plots . . . are handled without wit, without the humanity which is said to be the mark of Chaucer; often they trot to a climax so simple as to be non-existent.*
>
> *. . . Bawdy without irony, the dialogue delivered in elocution-class tones, naked buttocks protruding from every window, every aperture—it makes one wonder whether the alien setting it was which made one think the Decameron quite a film. Really, you know, Pasolini has reduced* The Canterbury Tales *to a series of bums and farts.*

It is sad that an age which has been one of a rediscovery of the oral tradition, which has made poetry into a living thing again for many people, should also be an age in which the pressures of box-office commercialism should reduce one of the greatest and most humane of poets in the English language to this kind of tawdry triviality. Chaucer himself, like a good many of his contemporaries, took hearty pleasure in bawdy stories, such as those told by the Miller and the Reeve. He intended not to shock but to amuse his readers, much as a modern comedian may pitch his more risky jokes so as to make his audience laugh, but not to shock them into silence. The bawdy tales, however, are few and although they show us a very characteristic side of Chaucer and his age, they do not represent the most typical qualities of his writing. But Chaucer has so far shown himself capable of surviving the worst treatment he has received at the hands of poetasters and media-mongers. The Chaucer industry has done its worst but it has not yet extinguished the delight we can find in 'God's plenty' even today.

Bibliography

FURTHER READING

BREWER, D. *Chaucer in his Time* (Longman, 1973) Social background to Chaucer's life and work.

CHUTE, M. *Geoffrey Chaucer of England* (Secker, 1946)

COULTON, C. G. *Chaucer and his England* (Methuen, 1965) The social and historical milieu of Chaucer's day.

HUSSEY, M. (Ed.) *Chaucer's World* (Camb. U.P., 1967) This 'pictorial companion' illustrates the lives and habits of Chaucer's pilgrims.

HUSSEY, M. (Ed.) *An Introduction to Chaucer* (Camb. U.P., 1965) Chaucer's life, his language, his poetry, the England of his day, the Church and medieval science.

POWER, E. *Medieval People* (Methuen, 1966) A series of portraits of people of the Middle Ages.

RICKERT, E. (Ed.) *Chaucer's World* (Columbia U.P., 1962) A collection of extracts from contemporary documents which illustrate life in Chaucer's England.

ROWLAND, B. *A Companion to Chaucer Studies* (O.U.P., 1968) An encyclopaedic general background book.

REFERENCE

General

BAINTON, R. H. *The Medieval Church* (Van Nost. Reinhold, 1963)

BENNETT, J. A. W. *Chaucer at Oxford and at Cambridge* (O.U.P., 1974)

HUIZINGA, J. *The Waning of the Middle Ages* (Penguin, 1972) A lively evocation of the religious, literary and artistic ideas in France and the Netherlands in Chaucer's day.

MATHEW, G. *The Court of Richard II* (J. Murray, 1968)

MYERS, A. R. *England in the Late Middle Ages* (Penguin, 1972) A short general history of England which considers economic, social, religious and educational developments as well as political events.

NORTON-SMITH, J.   *Geoffrey Chaucer* (Routledge, 1974)

OWST, G. R.   *Literature and the Pulpit in Medieval England* (Blackwell, 1961)

TREVELYAN, G. M.   *England in the Age of Wycliff* (Longman, 1972)

WADDELL, H.   *Medieval Latin Lyrics* (Constable, 1966)   Short Latin poems, with a verse translation on facing pages, which conveys some of the spirit of the original.

WOLEDGE, B. (Ed.)   *The Penguin Book of French Verse* vol. 1, *To the Fifteenth Century* (Penguin, 1968)   A collection of extracts from the work of some of the French poets Chaucer knew, with prose translations.

Medieval Science

CURRY, W. C.   *Chaucer and the Medieval Sciences* (Barnes & Noble, 1959)   A discussion of those of Chaucer's characters whose personalities display his knowledge of medieval sciences.

HOLMYARD, E. J.   *Alchemy* (Penguin, 1968)   A comprehensive study of medieval alchemy.

HUSSEY, M.   *An Introduction to Chaucer* (Camb. U.P., 1965) The final section of this book, by J. Winny, deals with Chaucer's knowledge of science and explains the medieval astronomical theories with which Chaucer would have been familiar.

LEWIS, C. S.   *The Discarded Image* (Camb. U.P., 1968)   An important discussion of the nature of the medieval picture of the world.

CRITICISM

ATKINS, J. W.   *English Literary Criticism: The Medieval Phase* (Camb. U.P., 1952)   Still one of the best books of its kind.

BREWER, D. S. (Ed.)   *Chaucer and the Chaucerians* (Nelson, 1970) A collection of essays by a variety of scholars on aspects of the work of Chaucer and the 'Chaucerians'.

COGHILL, N.   *The Poet Chaucer* (O.U.P., 1967)   A readable background book, with some critical material.

COGHILL, N.   *Geoffrey Chaucer* (Writers and their Work) (Brit. Council/Longman, 1956)

LEWIS, C. S.   *The Allegory of Love* (O.U.P., 1936)   In this very important work, C. S. Lewis is concerned less with *The Canterbury Tales* than with Chaucer's other works, but what he has to say is vital to an understanding of the background to Chaucer's thought.

PREMINGER, A. etc. *Classical and Medieval Literary Criticism* (New York, 1974) A collection of source material.

SALTER, E. *Chaucer's 'Knight's Tale' and 'Clerk's Tale'* (Studies in English Literature) (Ed. Arnold, 1962) Contains discussions of sources, language and style.

SPEARING, A. C. *Criticism and Medieval Poetry* (Ed. Arnold, 1972) A discussion of the problems which arise for the critic in applying the modern apparatus of criticism to poetry of the Middle Ages.

TRANSLATIONS

The Canterbury Tales tr. N. Coghill (Penguin, 1960) A verse translation, in which the problems of keeping to a verse form add to the difficulties which must arise in the attempt to render Chaucer's text exactly.

The Canterbury Tales tr. D. Wright (Barrie & Rockcliff, 1964) A helpful prose translation.

Chaucer Contemporaries

Piers Plowman William Langland tr. J. T. Goodridge (Penguin, 1970)

Confessio Amantis John Gower tr. T. Tiller (Penguin, 1969)

Sir Gawain and the Green Knight ed. B. Stone (Penguin, 1970)

AUDIO-VISUAL MATERIAL

The National Committee for Audio-Visual Aids in Education, 33 Queen Anne Street, London W1M 0AL, has published a series of multi-media kits to link with *Authors in Their Age*, consisting of filmstrip, cassette and notes. The Chaucer filmstrip has two main themes—European influences on Chaucer himself and how he has appeared to subsequent generations of readers.

Index